# RODGERS AND HAMMERSTEIN'S *Carousel*

*Oxford* KEYNOTES
*Series Editor* KEVIN C. KARNES

*Sergei Prokofiev's* Alexander Nevsky
KEVIN BARTIG

*Aaron Copland's* Appalachian Spring
ANNEGRET FAUSER

*Arlen and Harburg's* Over the Rainbow
WALTER FRISCH

*Arvo Pärt's* Tabula Rasa
KEVIN C. KARNES

*Beethoven's Symphony No. 9*
ALEXANDER REHDING

*Rodgers and Hammerstein's* Carousel
TIM CARTER

*Oxford* KEYNOTES

# RODGERS AND HAMMERSTEIN'S *Carousel*

TIM CARTER

Oxford University Press is a department of the University of Oxford. It furthers the University's objective of excellence in research, scholarship, and education by publishing worldwide. Oxford is a registered trade mark of Oxford University Press in the UK and certain other countries.

Published in the United States of America by Oxford University Press
198 Madison Avenue, New York, NY 10016, United States of America.



Library of Congress Cataloging-in-Publication Data
Names: Carter, Tim, 1954– author.
Title: Rodgers and Hammerstein's Carousel / Tim Carter.
Description: New York, NY : Oxford University Press, [2017] |
Series: Oxford keynotes | Includes bibliographical references and index.
Identifiers: LCCN 2017017870 | ISBN 9780190693435 (hardcover : alk. paper) |
ISBN 9780190693442 (pbk. : alk. paper)
Subjects: LCSH: Rodgers, Richard, 1902–1979. Carousel. |
Hammerstein, Oscar, II, 1895–1960.
Classification: LCC ML410.R6315 C39 2017 |
DDC 782.1/4—dc23
LC record available at https://lccn.loc.gov/2017017870

## *Series Editor's* INTRODUCTION

Oxford Keynotes reimagines the canons of Western music for the twenty-first century. With each of its volumes dedicated to a single composition or album, the series provides an informed, critical, and provocative companion to music as artwork and experience. Books in the series explore how works of music have engaged listeners, performers, artists, and others through history and in the present. They illuminate the roles of musicians and musics in shaping Western cultures and societies, and they seek to spark discussion of ongoing transitions in contemporary musical landscapes. Each approaches its key work in a unique way, tailored to the distinct opportunities that the work presents. Targeted at performers, curious listeners, and advanced undergraduates, volumes in the series are written by expert and engaging voices in their fields, and will therefore be of significant interest to scholars and critics as well.

In selecting titles for the series, Oxford Keynotes balances two ways of defining the canons of Western music: as lists of works that critics and scholars deem to have articulated key moments in the history of the art, and as lists of works that comprise the bulk of what consumers listen to, purchase, and perform today. Often, the two lists intersect, but the overlap is imperfect. While not neglecting the first, Oxford Keynotes gives considerable weight to the second. It confronts the musicological canon with the living repertoire of performance and recording in classical, popular, jazz, and other idioms. And it seeks to expand that living repertoire through the latest musicological research.

Kevin C. Karnes
Emory University

# CONTENTS

# ABOUT THE COMPANION WEBSITE

Oxford University Press has created a website to accompany *Rodgers and Hammerstein's Carousel* that features a variety of related multimedia materials, including audio clips for all in-text musical examples. Many of these resources are integral to the volume itself or provide needed and useful context. As with all of the websites for Oxford Keynotes volumes, the reader is encouraged to take advantage of this valuable online information to expand their experience beyond the print book in hand. Examples available online are indicated in the text with Oxford's symbol ▶.

www.oup.com/us/rhc
Username: Music4
Password: Book2497

The reader is invited to explore the full catalog of Oxford Keynotes volumes on the series homepage.
www.oup.com/us/oxfordkeynotes

# ACKNOWLEDGMENTS

I AM GRATEFUL TO Mark Eden Horowitz of the Music Division, Library of Congress, for guiding me to Oscar Hammerstein II's scenario for *Carousel* and for his constant willingness to help scholars working on American musical theater. Geoffrey Block, a mentor to so many of us in the field, was an important sounding board for my ideas, improving them along the way. Kim Kowalke, Jeffrey Magee, Bradley Rogers, and Charles Troy also shared materials and enthusiasm with me; András Nagy and István Várkonyi helped me through the bibliographical minefield of the early Hungarian and German versions of Molnár's *Liliom*; Tom Slater provided important information on the 1919 film *A Trip to Paradise*; and Brian Mitchell, archivist at the Houston Grand Opera, generously sent me the program of its 1990 production of *Carousel*.

Andrew Weaver and Mark Seto were kind enough to ask me to speak on the show in conjunction with fine student productions, respectively, at the Catholic University of America (October 2014) and Connecticut College (March 2016); it was the former invitation that prompted me to start my research. My writing was enabled by a fellowship at the National Humanities Center in 2015–16; the staff and other scholars there offered the perfect environment to bring it to fruition. Kevin Karnes was an expert series editor. My beloved wife and fiercest critic, Annegret Fauser, contributed more than I can say.

Tim Carter
Chapel Hill, NC
February 2017

# ARCHIVES AND SOURCES

My engagement with *Carousel* was aided by the exemplary revision of the vocal score supervised by Bruce Pomahac (New York: Williamson Music, 2000), which replaces the original 1945 piano-vocal score edited by Albert Szirmay. I also benefited from access to the Theatre Guild Archive in the Beinecke Rare Book and Manuscript Library, Yale University (B/TG), and to sources in the Library of Congress, Washington, DC, including the Oscar Hammerstein II Collection (LC/OH), Richard Rodgers Collection (LC/RR), and Rouben Mamoulian Papers (LC/RM). Articles in the press are cited by headline, newspaper (*NYT* = *New York Times*), and date. Quotations from Ferenc Molnár's play are taken from the English translation credited to Benjamin F. Glazer as *Liliom: A Legend in Seven Scenes and a Prologue* (New York: Boni & Liveright, 1921); those from the libretto of *Carousel* follow the text given in *Rodgers and Hammerstein's "Carousel": The Complete Book and Lyrics of the Broadway Musical* (Milwaukee, WI: Applause Theatre and Cinema Books, 2016), which supersedes the one in *Six Plays by Rodgers and Hammerstein* (New York: Random House, 1959), also with very slight differences from the revised vocal score.

# RODGERS AND HAMMERSTEIN'S *Carousel*

# CHAPTER 1

# *CAROUSEL* IN CONTEXT

RICHARD RODGERS AND OSCAR HAMMERSTEIN II's *Carousel* holds a special place in the history of the Broadway musical. It opened in New York's Majestic Theatre on April 19, 1945, and was an immediate success. *Carousel* also became Rodgers's personal favorite of his long series of collaborations with Hammerstein, which continued on a regular two-year cycle from *Oklahoma!* (1943) to *The Sound of Music* (1959). Moreover, while *Oklahoma!* has often been granted "landmark" status for its apparent "integration" of drama, music, and dance within a coherent plot, *Carousel* gains extra credit for its serious subject and seemingly operatic tendencies. The ill-fated marriage of Billy Bigelow, a carnival barker, and Julie Jordan, a mill worker, and then Billy's death and his chance at redemption during one day back on earth seem a far cry from all-singing, all-dancing Oklahoma cowboys and farmers. Not for nothing has *Carousel* tended to move beyond Broadway into the hallowed halls of high-art theater and opera.

For similar reasons, the show figures prominently in historical accounts of American musical theater. Ethan Mordden regards it as an "operetta by other means," while Larry Stempel treats it as a case study of the "new art" of musical theater. *Carousel* has a fine chapter ("The Invasion of the Integrated Musical") in Geoffrey Block's survey of the repertoire; Joseph Swain offers a detailed discussion of the show's "musical unity," albeit on somewhat dubious grounds; and for Scott McMillin, it is a prime example of "the musical as drama." All have influenced my account here. However, other noted scholars seem to be somewhat nonplussed by what to do with *Carousel*: it receives scant mention in texts such as those by Raymond Knapp and Stacy Wolf, which are now regarded, quite rightly, as having made a significant contribution to the revival of scholarly interest in the genre. This may well be to do with the show's troublesome subject matter, as we shall see.[1]

Both *Oklahoma!* and *Carousel* were produced by the Theatre Guild, with Lawrence Langner and Theresa Helburn at the helm (see figure 1.1). The Guild (established in 1919) had found its niche in the competitive world of Broadway by bringing to the stage classic and modern European repertoire as well as new American plays. It also garnered critical acclaim in 1935 when it produced George and Ira Gershwin's "folk opera" *Porgy and Bess*, an adaptation of Dorothy and DuBose Heyward's play *Porgy* done by the Guild in 1927. *Oklahoma!* was a result of submitting

FIGURE 1.1 Rouben Mamoulian, Oscar Hammerstein II, Theresa Helburn, and Richard Rodgers. Courtesy of Rodgers & Hammerstein: An Imagem Company, www.rnh.com

another Guild play, Lynn Riggs's *Green Grow the Lilacs* (1931), to similar musical treatment; the pattern continued with *Carousel*, based on *Liliom* (1909) by the Hungarian playwright Ferenc Molnár, which had been staged by the Guild in 1921. Indeed, at one point a musical *Liliom* was to be a direct successor to *Porgy and Bess* as Theresa Helburn entered into negotiations over it in 1937 with the German-Jewish refugee composer Kurt Weill, although their plans fell through because Molnár refused to release the play. He was more accommodating after he arrived in the United States as another Jewish refugee in 1939, but not before he saw a performance of *Oklahoma!*

Rodgers and Hammerstein's first show was an unexpected triumph; it also rescued the Guild from the financial difficulties facing many Broadway producers during World War II. Helburn knew that she had a successful creative team on hand: not just the composer and his new collaborator but also the director Rouben Mamoulian (who in addition had been involved in *Porgy and Bess*) and choreographer Agnes de Mille (see Table 1.1). But with *Oklahoma!* playing to sold-out houses at the St. James Theatre (246 W. 44th St.), it was clear that *Carousel*, directly across the street at the Majestic (247 W. 44th St.), needed to be different somehow.

The creators of *Oklahoma!* came together from quite different directions. Rodgers had secured a long run of Broadway successes with his constant partner, Lorenz Hart, whereas Hammerstein's reputation based on his work in the 1920s, including the classic *Show Boat* (with Jerome Kern) of 1927, was marred by a series of more recent flops. But Hart was drinking himself into an early death, and while *Oklahoma!* was meant to be a one-time deal, it soon became clear that a permanent Rodgers and Hammerstein partnership was in the cards. Yet they each had other projects to be completed before they could embark on another collaboration. A number of problems also emerged when they started considering a musical version of *Liliom* in late 1943. Rodgers later claimed that it was the potential of what became Billy Bigelow's "Soliloquy" that convinced them to take on the venture. But they had to resolve a number of dilemmas along the way, starting with whether and how to shift the action of Molnár's play from Budapest to America (eventually the New England coast). The process can be traced through Hammerstein's draft scenario—discussed here

TABLE 1.1 Production credits for *Oklahoma!* (St. James Theatre, March 31, 1943) and *Carousel* (Majestic Theatre, April 19, 1945)

| *Oklahoma!* | *Carousel* |
|---|---|
| ***Producers:*** | |
| The Theatre Guild (Theresa Helburn and Lawrence Langner) | The Theatre Guild (Theresa Helburn and Lawrence Langner) |
| ***Source:*** | |
| Lynn Riggs, *Green Grow the Lilacs* (produced by Theatre Guild in 1931) | Ferenc Molnár, *Liliom* (produced by Theatre Guild in 1921) |
| ***Director:*** | |
| Rouben Mamoulian | Rouben Mamoulian |
| ***Choreographer*:** | |
| Agnes de Mille | Agnes de Mille |
| ***Orchestrations:*** | |
| Robert Russell Bennett | Don Walker and others (Bennett orchestrated "The Carousel Waltz" and "Mister Snow" but then withdrew) |
| ***Scene design:*** | |
| Lemuel Ayers | Jo Mielziner |
| ***Costumes:*** | |
| Miles White | Miles White |
| ***Musical Director:*** | |
| Jay Blackton (Jacob Schwartzdorf) | Joseph Littau |

for the first time—and then what Rodgers, Hammerstein, Helburn, and Langner (and Molnár in the wings) did to *Carousel* as it moved into the tryouts in New Haven and Boston before the New York opening.

"Soliloquy" is one of several extended sequences in *Carousel* that distinguish the show still further from *Oklahoma!* or any other Broadway musical play. Such dramatic and musical weight was of particular concern during World War II in terms of what might define the seemingly elusive genre of "American" opera in contrast to the increasingly alien European works that dominated the repertoire. Rodgers and Hammerstein actively participated in a debate that was fostered by the prominent music critic of the *New York Times* Olin Downes, although Rodgers, at least, changed his tune several times as he sought to reconcile any such artistic pretensions with the demands of the "middlebrow" audiences that were the mainstay of the Broadway box office.

The arts played an important role in a country at war: the song "You'll Never Walk Alone" heard at the end of *Carousel* clearly contained an inspirational message. But it was also the dark subject matter of the show that seemed to take it in new directions. Billy Bigelow is feckless, maladjusted, and prone to violence, and Julie Jordan submits—willingly, it seems—to domestic abuse. The morale-boosting functions of *Oklahoma!* and its extolling of a land that is "grand" were much needed in 1943. With World War II now coming to a close, however, the US government was worrying more about the problems of reintegrating veterans into a civil society that had greatly changed in the meantime. Rodgers and

Hammerstein worked hard at the ending of *Carousel* so as to give Billy something denied him in Molnár's play: a clear resolution. But whether they made the right choice is another matter altogether.

Rodgers was proud of *Carousel*:

> Oscar never wrote more meaningful or more moving lyrics, and to me, my score is more satisfying than any I've ever written. But it's not just the songs; it's the whole play. Beautifully written, tender without being mawkish, it affects me deeply every time I see it performed.[2]

Nothing is so easy about the show, however, and to gloss over its problems would be to ignore precisely what it achieved. Digging beneath the surface raises a number of questions about how *Carousel* functions as musical drama, and what work it did in cultural, social, and political terms in 1945 (and has done since). This book seeks to answer them.

## CHAPTER 2

# MOLNÁR'S *LILIOM*

## *FROM BUDAPEST TO BROADWAY (AND BEYOND)*

FERENC MOLNÁR'S *LILIOM: EGY csirkefogó élete és halála—Külvárosi legenda hét képben* (Liliom: The life and death of a scoundrel—A suburban legend in seven tableaux) was his fourth play. It did not have much success in its first production in Budapest, opening on December 7, 1909: audiences were confused by its moral ambiguities, and the author took it off the stage after just a short run. It fared better in a German version by Alfred Polgar as *Liliom: Vorstadtlegende in 7 Bildern und einem szenischen Prolog* (Liliom: A suburban legend in seven tableaux and a scenic prologue), first done in Berlin in 1912: the "scenic prologue" was new, and other changes were made to the text, probably with Molnár's approval. The play took Vienna by storm when it was staged at the Theater in der Josefstadt on February 28, 1913. An English translation credited to Benjamin F. Glazer (*Liliom: A Legend in Seven Scenes and a Prologue*) was mounted on Broadway by the Theatre Guild on April 20, 1921, leading to what was, for the Guild, a long run of three hundred performances (to January 7, 1922). This was based on Polgar's text, though Glazer did not acknowledge that fact; nor did he admit that the bulk of the translation was done by Lorenz Hart (who was fluent in German). Thus it had the additions not present in the original Hungarian version, including the prologue and also the final lines for Julie and her daughter (about being beaten and it not hurting at all). But the Guild production helped confirm Molnár's stature as a leading European playwright: another fourteen of his plays appeared on Broadway in the 1920s and 1930s, plus a 1921 musical version of his *The Phantom Rival* (as *The Love Letter*) with music by Victor Jacobi and starring Fred and Adele Astaire.[1]

*Liliom* came to be regarded as one of Molnár's classics. Joseph Schildkraut and Eva Le Gallienne reprised their roles as Liliom and Julie in a Theatre Guild revival in 1932, with the role of Wolf Beifeld played by Howard Da Silva, who later was Larry Foreman in Marc Blitzstein's *The Cradle Will Rock* (1937) and Jud in *Oklahoma!* Orson Welles and Helen Hayes took the leads in a one-hour radio adaptation for the CBS *Campbell Playhouse* program broadcast on October 22, 1939. In 1940, Burgess Meredith and Ingrid Bergman headed a production that involved Molnár himself, who had arrived in the United States the year before (see figure 2.1), and Tyrone Power was Liliom in a run at the Westport Country Playhouse (Connecticut) in summer 1941, directed by Lee Strasberg. As Richard Rodgers later noted in his autobiography, the play "was continually being revived without any help from a songwriting team."[2] Not for nothing were he and Oscar Hammerstein II concerned about submitting so well-known a work to musical treatment.

In 1943, *Liliom* was included in an anthology of *Sixteen Famous European Plays* alongside works by Chekhov, Giraudoux, Ibsen, Pirandello, and others. In his preface, theater director John Anderson said that it was "one of the few fantasies in dramatic literature that has real iron in its soul." However, he claimed to have had some difficulty in identifying "the transcendent point of the play . . . that the

FIGURE 2.1 Burgess Meredith (Liliom), Vinton Freedley (producer), Ferenc Molnár, and Ingrid Berman (Julie) prepare the 1940 Broadway production of Molnár's *Liliom*. akg-images/TT News Agency/SVT

human spirit endures beyond the judgment of heaven and the pain of hell, and that in the mute and hurting passion of these two lovers, nothing here or hereafter shall save them from one another."[3] He might have found it easier had he known the subtitle of Molnár's original Hungarian version: *Egy csirkefogó élete és halála* (The life and death of a scoundrel)—the Hungarian *csirkefogó* also has a colloquial sense of a rogue who snatches "chickens" (women). Molnár's account of a low-life carousel barker in Budapest, Andreas Zavoczki, and his troubled relationship with Julie Zeller, a housemaid, engaged with the harsh life of an impoverished urban proletariat, also with what reads nowadays as some disconcerting ruminations on the actions of "good" and "bad" Jews (Molnár was Jewish).

Zavoczki (Billy Bigelow in *Carousel*) wears his nickname proudly: "Liliom" is Hungarian for "lily" but also slang for a tough, as was carefully explained in the 1921 edition of the English text. In the play, he first encounters Julie (Julie Jordan, a mill worker) at the fairground in a mimed prologue, and they then meet later in the park, by a bench under a flowering acacia tree. She is clearly attracted to him, as she has been to other men before, though never with the intent to marry. Liliom's employer, Mrs. Muskat (Mrs. Mullin), disapproves and fires him; Julie also deliberately loses her job by staying out late, ignoring the advice of her friend and fellow housemaid Marie (Carrie Pipperidge, who also works at the mill). Marie's prospects are on the rise: she is in love with Wolf Beifeld, a hotel porter (Enoch Snow, a fisherman).[4] Two months later, Liliom and Julie are now married and living off her aunt, Mrs. Hollunder, who runs a photographic studio (Nettie Fowler, proprietor of a seaside spa). But their relationship is going downhill: Liliom still fails, or refuses, to find a job, stays out night after night, has twice been arrested for brawling, and beats his wife. Julie's aunt advises her to drop him and marry the Carpenter, who would gladly have her hand (he is unnamed in the play and absent from *Carousel*). She still loves her husband, however, despite his abuse, which she excuses by his inability to find work. Mrs. Muskat offers Liliom his old job back, but Julie preempts any decision by announcing that she is pregnant.

Liliom is thrilled at the idea of becoming a father but then fears the financial consequences; he teams up with his dubious friend Ficsúr (Hungarian for "toff"; the character is called "The Sparrow" in the 1921 cast list and becomes Jigger Craigin in *Carousel*). They devise a harebrained scheme to steal the weekly payroll from the cashier of a leather factory, Linzman (David Bascombe, owner of the mill where Julie Jordan works). They will then flee to America. As they lie in wait by a railway embankment, Ficsúr cheats Liliom at cards, thereby claiming all the money from the robbery in advance. The deed itself then takes a bad turn: Linzman is not in fact carrying any money, and the police arrive. Ficsúr makes his escape, but Liliom is trapped and stabs himself to evade capture. He is brought back home on a stretcher and manages to utter some last words to Julie, explaining that he beat her not out of anger but because of his frustrations at his own inadequacies. He dies in her arms, and she declares her love for him over his body. The Carpenter enters to offer Julie help, but she politely declines (he then disappears from the plot). Two dark-suited men (they call themselves "God's police") place Liliom under arrest—suicide does not bring an end to things—and lead him off.

In "a courtroom in the beyond," the Magistrate offers Liliom the chance granted to all who cause their own death: to return to earth before sunrise to do what might have been left undone. He refuses, despite being reminded of his obligations to Julie and his unborn child (revealed to be a girl). The Magistrate is frustrated but sees some potential for repentance: he condemns Liliom to sixteen years in the "crimson fire," after which he will be allowed one day to see his daughter, when his actions will determine his eternal fate. Liliom makes a cocky exit, asking one of his guards for a cigarette as he leaves to begin his sentence.

In the final scene, set sixteen years later, Julie has found employment for herself and her daughter, Louise, in a jute factory. Marie and Wolf are moving up in the world: they have seven children, and Wolf is now proprietor of the Café Sorrento. Liliom enters accompanied by the two Heavenly Policemen; Julie thinks he is a beggar and offers him some soup. His attempts to engage with Louise fall flat, however: he tries to charm her with some card tricks, and then to give her a star stolen from heaven, but Louise refuses both. Liliom, frustrated once more, slaps her on the hand, though to Louise it feels like a caress. The silent Heavenly Policemen lead Liliom off to an unstated future. Louise still does not understand how she could be hit and have it not hurt her at all, but Julie says that it has happened to her, too. As the curtain falls, we hear the music of an organ grinder.

Molnár made use of music earlier in the play as well: the prologue is acted out over the bustle of a fairground, including the "strident music of a calliope" alongside "the signal bells of a merry-go-round," and the sounds of the carousel are heard again in the distance after Liliom has turned down Mrs. Muskat's offer of re-employment. As Ficsúr and Liliom plan their robbery, they hide it from Julie by breaking into strains of "The Thieves' Song," which recurs intertwined with the sounds of the carousel as Liliom is led off after his death; it then appears "in slow, altered tempo" as a trumpet fanfare for the courtroom scene. For the 1921 Theatre Guild production, the score was composed by Deems Taylor; it was reused in 1932 and 1940 but is now lost, it seems. The fact that music had such a thematic role in the play, however, probably had some impact on Theresa Helburn's thinking about a possible musical adaptation of *Liliom* both in 1937 and in 1943.

## THREE FILM VERSIONS

The revival of interest in *Liliom* in Hungary after World War I prompted plans for a silent-film version (in 1919), but it was abandoned in midstream as the director, Mihály Kertész (Michael Curtiz), left for Vienna after the declaration of the Hungarian Soviet Republic. The idea bore greater fruit in the United States as Metro Pictures released the silent *A Trip to Paradise* on September 5, 1921—while the play was still on Broadway—directed by Maxwell Karger and starring Bert Lytell as Curly Flynn (Liliom) and Virginia Valli as Nora O'Brien (Julie). The film is lost, but the surviving script, by June Mathis, shows that the action was transplanted to Coney Island. Mathis also switched things around considerably. Thus the robbery involves a house break-in interrupted by the owner and his daughter; Curly's accomplice, Jim Meek (Ficsúr), fires his revolver; and to save the girl, Curly steps in front of the shot, leaving him seriously wounded, though not dead. His heavenly judgment is treated as a subconscious fantasy as he undergoes surgery; his own good deed and Nora's prayers save the day. Curly recovers to live happily ever after, and the final scene (set later) shows him taking his wife and daughter on the carnival ride from which the film draws its title.[5]

Two sound films of *Liliom* stayed much closer to the play and to its European setting. The one released in the United States in October 1930 by Fox Film Corporation had a screenplay adapted by S. N. Behrman and Sonya Levien and was directed by Frank Borzage, with Charles Farrell as Liliom and Rose Hobart as Julie. It also had an innovative score by Richard Fall that used music sparsely but to great effect, especially by folding sections that are diegetic (from a "real" source, as from the carousel or a beer-garden band) into the underscoring to make dramatic points.[6] Better known, however, is Fox-Europa's French version of *Liliom*, released in May 1934, directed by Fritz Lang, with music by Jean Lenoir and Franz Waxman. This provided an early starring role for the young Charles Boyer, as well as allowing Madeleine Ozeray to play both Julie and her daughter. The screenplay by Robert Liebmann took a few liberties in adapting the play, including a new scene where Liliom encounters real-life bureaucrats who then reappear in similar roles in the beyond. Liebmann massaged the ending, too, as did Behrman and Levien for the 1930 version, so as to provide a clearer heavenly outcome for Liliom (as we shall see in chapter 5).

Fritz Lang thought it one of his best films.[7] We do not know whether Rodgers or Hammerstein saw it—it was released briefly in the United States in March 1935—but the composer Kurt Weill probably did during his time in Paris (1933–35) after fleeing the Nazis and before he moved across the Atlantic. However, he had already thought about a possible musical version of *Liliom* after seeing Karl Heinz Martin's production of the play in Berlin in 1928.

### *THE THEATRE GUILD, AMERICAN MUSICAL THEATER, AND A WOULD-BE* CAROUSEL

The production of Molnár's play at the Westport Country Playhouse in the summer of 1941 fits a pattern. The theater was run by Lawrence Langner and his wife, Armina Marshall, who were co-directors of the Theatre Guild alongside Theresa Helburn. Langner and Helburn also tended to use summer performances there as a way of reviving plays in which the Guild might have some further interest, and where they had some control over the rights: they staged Lynn Riggs's *Green Grow the Lilacs* there in 1940, and that production is often credited with prompting Helburn to consider reworking it as a musical play, which, after various twists and turns, became Rodgers and Hammerstein's first collaboration, *Oklahoma!* She may have come up with the idea because Riggs's play already featured a significant amount of music by way of cowboy songs. Something similar is true of the Theatre Guild's first such musical adaptation, George and Ira Gershwin's *Porgy and Bess*: Dorothy and DuBose Heyward's *Porgy* (itself adapted from DuBose Heyward's novel of 1925) contained a number of spirituals.

*Porgy and Bess* had already influenced Helburn's thinking on the possibilities of a musical *Liliom*, which she explored in a series of letters with Kurt Weill in February–May 1937.[8]

Pursuing creative ideas for the Guild was part of Helburn's job: her correspondence files are full of random suggestions that bore scant fruit. But she may have thought, at least for the moment, that *Liliom* had real possibilities, especially in the hands of a composer who seemed to fit the Guild's niche. Weill had arrived in the United States in September 1935 and was anxious to find opportunities on the New York stage that would build on his reputation within the European music-theatrical avant-garde following his collaborations in Berlin with Bertolt Brecht on *Die Dreigroschenoper* (*The Threepenny Opera*, 1928) and *Aufstieg und Fall der Stadt Mahagonny* (*Rise and Fall of the City of Mahagonny*, 1930). It was not easy. *The Threepenny Opera* had not gone down well in its brief Broadway run in 1933 save in left-wing circles, and Weill's first American works, *Johnny Johnson* (November 1936, in collaboration with the North Carolina playwright Paul Green) and the mammoth Jewish pageant *The Eternal Road* (January 1937), had both closed early. He went to Hollywood to seek better fortune, but with no greater success.

Weill was scrabbling around for projects that would provide him with some secure income, keeping as many balls in the air as he could. However, his ideas on a new kind of American musical theater situated somewhere between Broadway and opera would have appealed to Helburn, just as her suggestion of a musical *Liliom* did to him. As Weill wrote to her on February 15, 1937:

> The more I think about this idea, the more I feel that it would be absolutely ideal. I have now very definite ideas about it. I know what to do with the book, how to introduce the songs, in what

> style I would write and what form I would give it. The record of "Mahagonny" which I sent you will give you a little idea how I would conceive a musical version of "Liliom": with all kinds of music, spoken scenes, an orchester [*sic*] of not more than 16 pieces, no chorus, good singing actors (or good acting singers).

Weill went on to suggest possible actors to play the role of Liliom: Francis Lederer, Burgess Meredith, and, in a subsequent letter, James Cagney. He also proposed a director, Erik Charell (who had recently staged *White Horse Inn* on Broadway), who thought—so Weill claimed—that a musical *Liliom* would have the same outstanding success as *Die Dreigroschenoper*. Weill, too, may have sensed an affinity between the two works: *Die Dreigroschenoper* also dealt with low-life characters in dubious moral situations, and its lead roles, the blackguard Macheath (of "Mack the Knife" fame) and his on-off wife, Polly Peachum, have echoes in Liliom and Julie.

Invoking *Die Dreigroschenoper* may not have been the best argument to use with Helburn given its poor showing in New York in 1933. Nor was she very keen on Charell; instead she suggested Rouben Mamoulian (who had directed *Porgy and Bess*). Burgess Meredith, a friend of Weill's, could have seemed a decent idea: he had taken the role of Young Hollunder in the 1932 Theatre Guild revival of the play, and by 1936 he was playing Liliom in summer-stock productions, as he later did on Broadway in 1940. But what probably troubled Helburn most was her discovery that Weill was not being entirely open with her about having already sought Molnár's approval for a musical *Liliom* several years before. Molnár had turned Weill down then, as he had already done with Emmerich Kálmán and Franz Lehár, well-known composers of operettas, and even with the operatic maestro Giacomo Puccini.[9]

Weill persisted, suggesting that Helburn should adopt a two-pronged argument with Molnár: that the plan was not for "an opera but a play with songs and music," leaving the play itself intact, and that other dramatic works benefiting from such adaptation included Georg Büchner's *Woyzeck* (set by Alban Berg), Alexandre Dumas's *La Dame aux camélias* (Verdi's *La traviata*), George Bernard Shaw's *Arms and the Man* (Oscar Straus's *The Chocolate Soldier*), and Oscar Wilde's *Salome* (Richard Strauss). The reference to *Woyzeck* is revealing, given that it too concerns an antihero oppressed by economic circumstances and facing an unhappy end. But again, Weill made a slip: Helburn knew full well that Shaw was disgusted with *The Chocolate Soldier*, which is why he had refused to release his *Pygmalion* to Franz Lehár in 1921 (though much later it became *My Fair Lady*). Nevertheless, Helburn tried her best with Molnár, then conveyed to Weill with some regret his refusal (made through his agent) once more to release his play.

Weill pursued other possibilities with Helburn for the rest of the decade, none of which came to fruition. Later, he was grouchy about the favorable publicity given to *Carousel* for defining a new direction for musical theater.[10] Nor did it help that his *The Firebrand of Florence*, which opened on March 22, 1945 (the same day as the first New Haven tryout of *Carousel*), closed nine days after Rodgers and Hammerstein's new show reached Broadway. By then, Weill already had other successes under his belt, including *Lady in the Dark* (1941) and *One Touch of Venus* (1943). But his grumpiness was also due to the fact that Rodgers and Hammerstein's *Oklahoma!* had already been breaking box-office records for almost two years.

## *MOLNÁR SEES* OKLAHOMA!

When Helburn began seriously exploring the possibilities of a musical version of Lynn Riggs's *Green Grow the Lilacs* in late April or early May 1942, she was uncertain whether it would be a cowboy show (with music by the likes of Tex Ritter or Woody Guthrie), something more serious (by Aaron Copland or Roy Harris), or a way to bring the Broadway greats into the Guild fold: Richard Rodgers and Lorenz Hart were at the top of a list that also included Irving Berlin, Jerome Kern, and Cole Porter. Even Kurt Weill was briefly in the frame once more, although Helburn dismissed the idea early on. Rodgers came on board in mid-June, and on July 23, 1942, the *New York Times* reported the Theatre Guild's announcement the previous day that Rodgers and Hart would start work on the show, also in collaboration with Oscar Hammerstein II. This was a face-saving fiction, given that Hart was too ill to work. But Rodgers was not willing to abandon his longtime collaborator, however unreliable he had become, and what became *Oklahoma!* was just a diversion, so the story went, while Rodgers and Hart took time to plan their next great show. Hammerstein was willing to play along, in part out of generosity and in part because he needed a boost to his career following his own embarrassing series of flops.[11]

No one involved in *Oklahoma!* thought, at least at first, that it would take off as it did. During the fraught four weeks of rehearsals (the standard period allowed by contract), the director, Rouben Mamoulian, and the choreographer, Agnes de Mille, fought incessantly over who was responsible for what. The three-day tryout in New Haven, followed by two weeks in Boston, made everyone sick from exhaustion because of late-night rewriting and frantic restaging. The Broadway opening of *Oklahoma!* at the St. James Theatre on March 31, 1943, allowed Helburn and her colleagues to breathe more easily, however: it was an artistic triumph that set the cash registers ringing, while also boosting the morale of a nation at war. Rodgers and Hammerstein gave press interviews extolling the virtues of their "new" integration of drama and music, and they argued fiercely with Mamoulian over his own claims of having created it. But all reveled in the plaudits coming from far and wide, including the fact that Olin Downes, the important music critic of the *New York Times*, strayed from his usual turf to pen an appreciation headlined "Broadway's Gift to Opera" (it appeared on June 6), writing that *Oklahoma!* "shows one of the ways to an integrated and indigenous form of American lyric theatre." Helburn was no doubt delighted to have encouraged him to see the show, just as she was happy to respond to Downes's request (made to Hammerstein) for tickets for such other musical luminaries as Arturo Toscanini and Vladimir Horowitz. She also arranged reduced prices for soldiers shipping out to the front. But she did not forget another important invitation she needed to make: Ferenc Molnár saw *Oklahoma!* on October 21, 1943. The Guild also dangled another carrot, offering to stage Molnár's new play, *Noah's Ark*, in the current season (it never did). But given the timing, Helburn clearly had an ulterior motive: that performance of *Oklahoma!* is what prompted Molnár to change his mind over *Liliom*—the very next day, it seems—and to grant Rodgers and Hammerstein what he had refused to so many others.[12]

## CHAPTER 3

# CREATING *CAROUSEL*

EXCITEMENT IN THE Theatre Guild offices over *Oklahoma!* was tempered by caution. On July 31, 1943, the Guild's chief play reader, John Gassner, warned Theresa Helburn and Lawrence Langner that it would be a mistake for them to depend entirely on Richard Rodgers now that their success might enable them to recruit the likes of Irving Berlin and Jerome Kern as well—or instead. Gassner also suggested returning to Kurt Weill (to produce a musical version of Brecht's *Der gute Mensch von Sezuan*), and he listed sixty-three plays that might be adapted to music (fifty-four American and nine foreign), including William Saroyan's *The Time of Your Life* (1939, for Jerome Kern), Elmer Rice's *Street Scene* (1929; Weill later set it in 1946), and *Liliom*. This concern over Rodgers was in part a case of hedging bets, but it also arose from the question of his intended professional relationship with Oscar Hammerstein II. They had already been commissioned to write the songs for the film musical *State Fair* (the Guild also briefly considered a stage version of it), but Rodgers was reluctant to cement any permanent association while Lorenz Hart was still alive. His last act of loyalty to his former collaborator was to revive their 1927 musical *A Connecticut Yankee* (it opened on November 17, 1943). Meanwhile, Hammerstein was preoccupied with completing a long-time project adapting Bizet's opera *Carmen* as an African American *Carmen Jones* (premiered on December 2).[1]

Hart's death on November 22, 1943, removed one obstacle, and Rodgers and Hammerstein's new partnership was sufficiently well known in insider circles soon thereafter, even if it was not acknowledged in public until the middle of 1944 or thereabouts, when Rodgers told a reporter, "We have no plans that don't include each other." Helburn stuck to her guns, however. Having ensured Molnár's approval for a musical *Liliom* in late October 1943, she prepared a contract for Rodgers and Hammerstein sometime in November. It upped the ante significantly: they would jointly receive 7.5 percent of the weekly gross (it was 7 percent for *Oklahoma!*) plus an additional 40 percent of the Theatre Guild's share of the profits once investors had been paid; Molnár was given just 0.8 percent of the gross (less than Lynn Riggs's 1 percent for *Oklahoma!*). Given the timing, Hammerstein was sensitive enough to shift the chronology when he gave interviews in the run-up to *Carousel*, saying that he and Rodgers began work on it in January 1944. But their first formal production meeting with Helburn and Langner in fact took place on

December 7, 1943, exactly two weeks after Hart's death, and their second, on January 20, 1944. They signed their contract for *Liliom* in February, and the project was announced in the *New York Times* on March 1. But Langner was premature when he stated later that *Liliom* would be done in fall 1944, and likewise Rodgers, who suggested "some time next winter."[2]

### SOME DILEMMAS

What convinced Rodgers and Hammerstein of the viability of a musical *Liliom* at that first production meeting was the potential of what became Billy Bigelow's "Soliloquy," on the prospect of his becoming a father. But they still had a number of significant concerns about whether they could properly handle what was widely regarded as a "classic." The Hungarian setting, too, remained a problem: Hammerstein felt that it smacked too much of the faux exoticism typical of operetta—with corny csárdás dances and dreary costumes—and that it also raised issues because of the war (Hungary was officially on the side of the Axis). Helburn proposed shifting the location to Louisiana; Hammerstein resisted because it would be too hard to capture the Creole dialect (too many "zisses and zoses," he said). By February 1944, they had agreed on setting the show in New England instead.[3]

There were other anxieties in play here, however. Hammerstein had already explored the South in *Show Boat* (Mississippi) and *Carmen Jones* (North Carolina), and a New Orleans setting had not served well for his 1941 flop with Sigmund Romberg, *Sunny River*. Going regional—and pastoral rather than urban—was not itself a problem: as *Oklahoma!* had shown, it generated local color and helped justify the presence of music. But one further "southern" work, and perhaps a second, seem to have caused Hammerstein greater concern.

George and Ira Gershwin's *Porgy and Bess* (1935), set in Charleston, South Carolina, repeatedly exerts its presence as a subtext within *Carousel*. Hammerstein professed admiration for its revision by Cheryl Crawford in 1941–42 as a musical play, with spoken dialogue replacing the musical recitative: it ran on Broadway in January–September 1942, September–October 1943, and February–April 1944.[4] But he clearly worried about its impact on his own claims for a new form of musical theater dating back to *Show Boat* (1927). The 1936 film version of his and Jerome Kern's trailblazing show followed hard on the heels of the 1935 *Porgy and Bess*, and Crawford's revision urged Hammerstein to pursue a return of *Show Boat* to Broadway in 1942–43 (which did not happen); it also had an impact on *Carmen Jones*. Even *Carousel* could not escape the influence: there are obvious comparisons to be made between their problematic antiheroes and their "mimed" openings (although the "Jasbo Brown" one in *Porgy and Bess* had been dropped), while the offshore clambake and treasure hunt opening act 2 of *Carousel* serve a similar purpose to, and have strong dramatic echoes of, the picnic scene on Kittiwah Island in *Porgy and Bess*, act 2, scene 2.

There was also another musical play set "somewhere in the South" that had caused a stir at its opening on Broadway on October 25, 1940: Vernon Duke, John La Touche, and Lynn Root's *Cabin in the Sky*. Metro-Goldwyn-Mayer released a film version in April 1943. That show dealt with yet another antihero, "Little Joe" Jackson, who on his "death" in a fracas over gambling debts is given a divine reprieve for six months to do enough good deeds for his faithful wife, Petunia, so as to gain admission to heaven, though Lucifer Jr. puts temptations in his path in the form of the seductive temptress Georgia Brown. In the end (at least, in the film), it all turns out to have been Little Joe's dream—he had only been knocked unconscious—but the experience is sufficient to prompt repentance and reform. The parallels with *Liliom* are striking. But there was one key difference from Molnár's play. *Cabin in the Sky*, like *Porgy and Bess* before it, broke new ground by being written specifically for an African American cast.

Hammerstein was not color-blind; he was a staunch supporter of progressive causes and a highly active member of the NAACP, and he was already contributing to diversity on the Broadway stage by way of his all-black *Carmen Jones*, as he had previously done with *Show Boat*. Shifting *Liliom* to an all-white community on the "New England coast" between 1873 and 1888, however, brought a different set of resonances into play. New England could have meant any number of things to him and Rodgers, whether an idyllic rurality (Thoreau's *Walden, or Life in the Woods*) or puritanical small-town hypocrisy (Hawthorne's *The Scarlet Letter*)—there are elements of both in *Carousel*. Or perhaps they were reminded of yet another play that dealt with someone returning from the afterlife to present a moral lesson: Thornton Wilder's *Our Town* (1938, filmed with a different ending in 1940), set in the fictional Grover's Corners, New Hampshire. But the choice also represented a different approach to the issue that Olin Downes had already raised in his *New York Times* essay on *Oklahoma!*—that of creating an "integrated and indigenous form of American lyric theatre." This was a recurring theme: Downes had also broached it in his first encounter with *Porgy and Bess*, although by 1943 he thought that the Gershwins' folk opera was "not important at all," largely, it seems, because of its race-specific content and style. For better or for worse, he was far more comfortable with the simple "American folks" that Rodgers and Hammerstein proposed to put on the stage in *Carousel*.[5]

There is also another potential subtext here. The generic "New England coast" specified in the libretto to *Carousel* is, in fact, Maine, to judge by passing references in the libretto (e.g., to Penobscot and Augusta in the song "June Is Bustin' Out All Over"). Maine was also the focus of Hammerstein's preliminary research into literary and other sources as he set to work, from which he derived some of the new names for the characters of *Liliom* and also other plot matters.[6] But the choice brought problems in its wake. In the case of Maine, or even New England, there are no strong musical markers in the manner of the American South (spirituals) or Southwest (cowboy songs). Nor was there much room in *Carousel* for the kind of down-home Americana that Rodgers and Hammerstein were writing for the Iowa farmers in *State Fair*, although "A Real Nice Clambake" and "June Is Bustin' Out All Over" come close (each has strong, if different, echoes of one of the main songs of the film, "It's a Grand Night for Singing").[7] But the main attempt to provide local color in *Carousel*, by way of the song "Blow High, Blow Low," leads to the very odd situation of a carnival barker from Coney Island singing of the delights of whaling. The harbor setting may have been a strong enough reason for the song: designer Jo Mielziner's backdrops for the original *Carousel* sets make prominent use of a tall-masted sailing ship looming over the scene (see figure 3.1). Rodgers and Hammerstein may have had a further agenda here, however, given what immediately comes to mind: the "great American novel," Herman Melville's *Moby-Dick* (1851). *Carousel* may have had its roots in a Hungarian play, but it was in the end to be a genuinely American work, and perhaps even a "great" one at that.

## HAMMERSTEIN'S DRAFT SCENARIO

The most immediate competition faced by *Carousel*, however, came from *Oklahoma!*—Rodgers and Hammerstein's new show at the Majestic Theatre clearly needed to be different from their sellout success playing at the St. James, across the street. Thus the Theatre Guild allocated *Carousel* a much higher production budget—at $160,000, close to twice that *Oklahoma!* ($82,000 by one estimate)—and sought other ways to distinguish the two works.[8]

In one sense, Molnár's play seemed ready-made for a Broadway musical, which is no doubt what helped attract Theresa Helburn to it in the first place. Thus its characters are a close match to those of *Oklahoma!* (the parallels are laid out in Table 3.1) and other shows of the same kind: a strong male and female lead (Liliom and Julie), a second couple (Marie and Wolf), a matriarchal figure (Mrs. Hollunder, Julie's aunt), and a "heavy" (Ficsúr). One obvious difference was that Liliom (Billy Bigelow) is a much more troubled,

FIGURE 3.1 Billy Bigelow's death scene in *Carousel* (1945). Courtesy of Rodgers & Hammerstein: An Imagem Company, www.rnh.com

TABLE 3.1 Principal characters (and casting) of *Oklahoma!* and *Carousel*

| *Oklahoma!* | *Carousel* |
|---|---|
| Curly McClain (Alfred Drake) | Billy Bigelow (John Raitt) |
| Laurey Williams (Joan Roberts) | Julie Jordan (Jan Clayton) |
| Ado Annie Carnes (Celeste Holm) | Carrie Pipperidge (Jean Darling) |
| Will Parker (Lee Dixon) | Enoch Snow (Eric Mattson) |
| Aunt Eller (Betty Garde) | Nettie Fowler (Christine Johnson) |
| Jud Fry (Howard Da Silva) | Jigger Craigin (Murvyn Vye) |
| Ali Hakim (Joseph Buloff) | — |
| — | Louise (Bambi Linn) |

and troubling, character than Curly in *Oklahoma!* Also, Marie (Carrie Pipperidge) is less of a comic foil than Ado Annie, although she is more empty-headed in the play than she turns out in the show. Other questions were whether room could be made for a "specialty" song-and-dance man (such as Lee Dixon, who played Will Parker in *Oklahoma!*) or a comedian (Joseph Buloff as Ali Hakim). Of course, given the plot of *Liliom*, such lighter elements were likely to be in short supply. But it was a matter of some anxiety. For example, in the very early thinking on *Carousel*, with the setting still in Europe, Lawrence Langner thought that the idea of Liliom and Julie moving to America would allow some excellent opportunities for comedy. Rodgers, on the other hand, considered it a good basis for a song (for Julie, dreaming of what she might find there) and even for some kind of dream ballet.[9] This was far too close to *Oklahoma!* and too much of a distraction from the play.

Matters soon went in a different direction, to judge by a typed scenario reflecting Rodgers and Hammerstein's developing plans for the show (see the appendix). This was probably prepared in the summer of 1944,[10] and Hammerstein later described how such a document fit into their manner of working:

> Dick and I stay very close together while drawing up the blueprint of a play. Before we start to put words or notes on paper we have agreed on a very definite and complete outline, and we have decided how much of the story shall be told in dialogue and how much in song.[11]

Thus the scenario is a typical work-in-progress document that maps out the show, combining a list of scenes with locations, brief descriptions of the action, and notes on the intended music.

Although the scenario retains the original names for the characters, we are no longer in Budapest—the place is not yet specified, but the scenes are situated much as in the final version—and Julie and Marie work in a textile mill rather than as housemaids. A good deal of the action is set in place, which is not surprising for those portions based most closely on the play. However, things are fuzzy where Hammerstein deviated from it. Thus it is not yet clear whether the Mill Owner (Mr. Bascombe in *Carousel*) is the man robbed by Liliom and Ficsúr. That fuzziness is even greater in a new scene—the added treasure hunt on an island toward the beginning of act 2—and also in the case of how Hammerstein proposed handling Liliom's post-death experience (in the presence of Mr. and Mrs. God).

But he already knew the broad outline of another addition to the play, the final graduation scene. From Liliom's death on, he was trying to solve problems in the play that had to be addressed for the purposes of a musical adaptation, whether to sort out the dramatic action or just to provide appropriate opportunities for reprises. The new scene on the island, however, served a double purpose. First, it was a conventional, if quiet, act opener for the full ensemble, which was something required of a musical though not of a spoken play. Second, it was a result of a surprising plan to create a competing love interest for Marie: the guitar-playing Dwight, who is more attractive yet less reliable than the stodgy Wolf Beifeld. The island scene was when she would have to choose between the two of them.

The sequence of intended musical numbers for *Liliom* is clear enough: those in the scenario and the final version are placed side by side in Table 3.2. Sometimes the proposed titles match the final version: "June Is Bustin' Out All Over" appears at the opening of scene 3 (though the main singer is the mill owner, a speaking role in *Carousel*)—also with some idea for the lyrics—then as the finale to act 1, and in act 2 as the crowd returns from the island. Other numbers have different titles but the same function, as with "The Wind Blows the Blossoms" ("If I Loved You") and "I'm Going to Have a Baby!" (Billy's "Soliloquy"). This is also the case with "Sea Chanty" ("Blow High, Blow Low") and "Put Your Faith in Sardines and Me" ("When the Children Are Asleep"), although their positions are reversed. Still other songs are presented in vaguer terms, such as the "Female Duet" for Mrs. Hollunder (Nettie Fowler) and Julie over

TABLE 3.2 Musical numbers in the scenario and final version of *Carousel*

| Scenario | Final version |
|---|---|
| 1.1: ***Merry-go-round*** | 1.1: ***An amusement park on the New England Coast. May.*** |
| "Waltz Suite" | "Prologue: The Carousel Waltz" |
| 1.2: ***Park—or a path near the shore*** | 1.2: ***A tree-lined path along the shore. A few minutes later.*** |
| "What's on Your Mind?" (Marie, Julie, women) | "Mister Snow (Julie and Carrie Sequence)" |
| "The Wind Blows the Blossoms" (Liliom, Julie) | "If I Loved You" (Billy, Julie) |
| 1.3: ***Pier restaurant*** | 1.3: ***Nettie Fowler's spa on the ocean front. June.*** |
| "Bustin' Out All Over!" (Mill Owner, chorus) followed by "Sand Dance" | "June Is Bustin' Out All Over" (Carrie, Nettie, chorus) followed by "Girls' Dance" |
| "Just As If It Happened to Me" (Mrs. Hollunder) | |
| "Sea Chanty" (Ficsúr, Liliom, men) | [= "Blow High, Blow Low," below] |
| | "Reprise: Mister Snow" (Carrie, women) |
| "Put Your Faith in Sardines and Me" (Wolf, Marie) | "When the Children Are Asleep" (Carrie and Mr. Snow Sequence)" |
| | "Blow High, Blow Low" (Jigger, Billy, men) followed by "Hornpipe" |
| "That's My Idea of a Man" (Marie, Julie, Mrs. Muskat, Mrs. Hollunder) | |
| "I'm Going to Have a Baby!" (Liliom) | "Soliloquy" (Billy) |
| "Finale: Bustin' Out All Over" | "Finale: Act I" ("June Is Bustin' Out All Over") |

TABLE 3.2 Continued

| *Scenario* | *Final version* |
| --- | --- |
| 2.1: ***Island*** | 2.1: ***On an island across the bay. That night.*** |
| "A Song Drifts Over the Bay" (Ensemble and principals) | "A Real Nice Clambake" (Nettie, Julie, Enoch, Carrie, chorus) |
| "Here's What I Can Give You" (Marie, Wolf, Dwight) | |
| | "Geraniums in the Winder" (Enoch), leading to "Stonecutters Cut It on Stone" (Jigger, chorus) |
| "Finaletto" | "What's the Use of Wond'rin'?" (Julie, women) |
| 2.2: ***Culvert*** | 2.2: ***Mainland waterfront. An hour later.*** |
| Possible "mystic" number | |
| 2.3: ***Pier restaurant*** | |
| "Reprise: Bustin' Out All Over" | ("June is Bustin' Out All Over" cued in script for villagers' return) |
| "Female Duet" (Mrs. Hollunder, Julie) | "You'll Never Walk Alone" (Nettie, Julie, chorus) |
| | "The Highest Judge of All" (Billy) |
| 2.4: ***In transit*** | |
| Ballet | |
| 2.5: ***Front parlor*** | 2.3: ***Up there*** |
| "Life Is As Simple As You Make It" (Mr. and Mrs. God, Liliom) | |
| | 2.4: ***Down here. On a beach. Fifteen years later.*** |
| | "[Louise's] Ballet" |

(continued)

TABLE 3.2 Continued

| Scenario | Final version |
|---|---|
| 2.6: ***Louise's bedroom*** | 2.5: ***Outside Julie's cottage*** |
| | "Carrie's Incidental: I'm a Tomboy" |
| Reprises (as yet undecided) | "Porch Scene (Reprise: If I Loved You)" (Billy) |
| 2.7: ***Outside a schoolhouse—on the lawn*** | 2.6: ***Outside a schoolhouse. Same day.*** |
| "Graduation Song: Finale" | "Finale Ultimo (Reprise: You'll Never Walk Alone)" |

The 1945 layout of *Carousel* treated the prologue as an unnumbered scene ("Prelude"), meaning that act 1 has just two scenes; the vocal score implies three (the orchestral number immediately prior to "Mister Snow" is labeled "Opening Act I—Scene 2").

Liliom's dead body, which became "You'll Never Walk Alone." Nor does the scenario yet connect that duet with the "Graduation Song" at the end of act 2.

Numbers in the scenario that have no direct match in *Carousel* include two in act 1, scene 3, one for Mrs. Hollunder and the other a quartet for Marie, Julie, Mrs. Muskat (Mrs. Mullin), and Mrs. Hollunder as they state what they wish for in a man; a trio in act 2, scene 1, for Marie, Wolf, and Dwight as Marie works out which one to marry; a "mystic" number for the robbery scene in act 2, scene 2 (followed by underscoring for Liliom and Ficsúr's card game synchronized to their gestures); and in act 2, scene 5, a "simple little song" for Mr. and Mrs. God and Liliom. The act 2 ballet is also in a different position to depict Liliom "in transit," and it covers seventeen years of events on earth (including Ficsúr being hanged) rather than just Louise's travails as a teenager.[12] Songs in the final *Carousel* not present in any recognizable form in the scenario—we shall see why—are the sequence during the treasure hunt (leading to "What's the Use of Wond'rin'?") and also Billy's "The Highest Judge of All."

Given that the island scene and its business with Marie and Dwight were new to *Liliom*, Hammerstein noted in the scenario parallel situations in other well-known plays, including George Bernard Shaw's *Candida* (1894) and Edmond Rostand's *Cyrano de Bergerac* (1897); he also thought that its opening number (eventually "A Real Nice Clambake") should be a "Just a Song at Twilight" type, referring to James Lynam Molloy's well-known parlor favorite "Love's Old Sweet Song." For the proposed quartet in act 1, scene 3, Hammerstein referred to Sigmund Romberg's *The Desert Song* (1926), an operetta on which he had collaborated with Otto Harbach and Frank Mandel for the book and lyrics. This, in turn, is not quite what one might expect of a Broadway musical in the 1940s. Indeed, that quartet and the multiple duets and trios proposed in the scenario—plus the surprisingly few solo numbers (only two)—give *Carousel* as configured here a very different feel from *Oklahoma!* So does the fact that a great deal of dramatic action is allocated to these ensembles. The proportions shifted in the final version, which dropped the trios and the quartet and added solos for Julie ("What's the Use of Wond'rin'?") and Billy ("The Highest Judge of All"), though Mrs. Hollunder lost her song (Nettie Fowler takes the place of the mill owner in "June Is Bustin' Out All Over" instead). But Rodgers and Hammerstein's second show was clearly intended to be more musically ambitious than their first.

The need for *Carousel* to be demonstrably different from *Oklahoma!* probably explains why the hapless Dwight was removed from the Marie-Wolf subplot: a secondary love-triangle played a comic role in the earlier show as Ado Annie tries to decide between the stolid Will Parker and the exotic peddler Ali Hakim. But this left Marie/Carrie at something of a loose end. To fill the gap in the treasure-hunt scene, Hammerstein drew, consciously or not, on the picnic scene in *Porgy and Bess*, where Bess goes off with Crown on Kittiwah Island: Jigger Craigin flirts with Carrie and then tries to carry her off, and Enoch Snow catches them in the act, leading to him lamenting the collapse of all his domestic dreams ("Geraniums in the Winder").

Dwight had been dropped by the time of two draft scripts of *Carousel* that survive, one dated November 27, 1944 (just with act 1, scenes 1–2, but including lyrics), and another from January 9, 1945.[13] They clearly reflect Rodgers's work on the musical score. Much of the show had by now reached something close to its final form, without the quartet in act 1 and the solo number for Mrs. Hollunder. (The equivalent matriarchal figure in *Oklahoma!*, Aunt Eller, had also lost an act 1 song as that show went into rehearsal.) The act 2 ballet stays where it was in the scenario (just after Billy's death) but focuses more on Louise's growing up. The scene in God's front parlor now has no musical number, although Mrs. God plays "My boy, Bill!" softly on her harmonium as the lights fade, the orchestra then picking it up "loudly and buoyantly" as the link to the next scene "outside Julie's cottage" (according to the list at the front of the draft script, though at the head of the scene itself it is "outside a crude little seaside shack"). The main song still missing is Billy's

"The Highest Judge of All," which was added still later in rehearsal (although it picks up on a line already in the script) in order to give him a significant musical number in the act.

### CASTING, REHEARSALS, AND TRYOUTS

The change of title from *Liliom* to *Carousel* was noted in newspapers toward the beginning of January 1945, although there was some debate over the appropriate spelling (whether or not as *Carrousel*). Likewise, reports circulated around this time that Rouben Mamoulian had signed his contract as director, as he did on December 27, 1944, although he and the Guild had been in discussions about it since August, if not before. He received the same initial fee as for *Oklahoma!* ($3,500) but was able to increase his share of the gross receipts from 1 to 1.5 percent (then 2 percent after the production costs were paid off). Agnes de Mille had been linked to the *Liliom* project since June 1944, although her contract was fixed only later in November (and signed on February 9, 1945) as she argued for something better than what she had garnered for *Oklahoma!* (which had long been a bone of contention): her $4,500 fee plus 0.5 percent of the gross was a significant improvement. The main questions remaining concerned the musical director—Joseph Littau was brought in at the end of his run with *Carmen Jones*—and the likely cast. Some auditions had already been held—Mamoulian attended a session on 21 December—although the emerging musical demands of the score for *Carousel* were creating some dilemmas in terms of casting.[14]

FIGURE 3.2 Jan Clayton (Julie Jordan) and John Raitt (Billy Bigelow) in *Carousel* (1945). Courtesy of Rodgers & Hammerstein: An Imagem Company, www.rnh.com

John Raitt was already identified as a potential Liliom in spring 1944, and both Rodgers and Langner later said that discovering him was a key moment in the development of the show (see figure 3.2). Meanwhile, the Guild cast him (from May 1944) as Curly in the national company of *Oklahoma!* currently playing in Chicago. By the time of Hammerstein's scenario, another *Oklahoma!* graduate (from the premiere), the dancer Bambi Linn, had been identified to play Louise, and a third came later: Murvyn Vye (Jigger Craigin) had stepped in as Jud Fry on Broadway. However, in mid-January 1945, Theresa Helburn was in Hollywood still seeking out potential cast members for *Carousel*, and announcements of the performers started appearing in newspapers only in early February, very close to the start of rehearsals.[15]

Part of the problem was finding singers who could cope with roles far more demanding vocally than those of *Oklahoma!* The cast biographies in the *Carousel* program books made a virtue of it. John Raitt had sung in opera (in *Carmen*, *The Marriage of Figaro*, and *The Barber of Seville*), and Eric Mattson (Enoch Snow) was known for taking principal tenor roles in a wide range of operettas. Christine Johnson (Nettie Fowler) was even more an opera singer, having made her debut at the Metropolitan Opera in February 1944 as Erda in Wagner's *Der Ring des Nibelungen*; her other roles included Maddalena (in Verdi's *Rigoletto*) and Azucena (his *Il trovatore*). She was clearly underused in the final version of *Carousel*. The one relatively unknown member of this musically proficient cast was Jan Clayton (Julie Jordan); following some minor film roles, she was making her Broadway debut. However, Hammerstein may have seen her in a production of his and Jerome Kern's *Music in the Air*, perhaps at the Muny in St. Louis (Missouri) in 1944; after *Carousel* she played Magnolia in the 1946 revival of *Show Boat*.[16]

*Carousel* was further along than *Oklahoma!* had been when it went into rehearsal. Clearly Rodgers, Hammerstein, and the Theatre Guild learned a number of lessons from the first show they did together. So did Rouben Mamoulian and Agnes de Mille concerning how best to get along: Rodgers later claimed that it was far easier to work with them on *Carousel*, although de Mille detected some deterioration in her relations with the composer, which would get still worse. The customary four weeks of rehearsal starting on Monday, February 19, 1945, appear to have gone smoothly enough, and confidence was running high: Rodgers and Hammerstein announced their next collaboration, *Allegro*, at the start of rehearsals, and tickets for the first tryout performances of *Carousel* at the Shubert Theatre in New Haven sold out well in advance.[17]

As in the case of *Oklahoma!*, the Guild took *Carousel* to New Haven (Thursday–Saturday, March 22–24, 1945; four performances including a matinée), and then a run at the Colonial Theatre in Boston (Tuesday March 27 to Saturday April 14). Such tryouts were standard practice to iron out the kinks in a show before a Broadway opening. Typically, not much could be done in New Haven, which would be the first time the cast worked with full sets, costumes, and an orchestra. A longer run in Boston, however, permitted greater changes if needed, and it was probably the Guild's experience with *Oklahoma!* there that prompted a three-week booking, rather than two, for *Carousel*. It was common to have to cut shows down to bring their running time to a reasonable length, something that could only be gauged in a full staging, as well as to build on audience responses on matters of content and pacing.

As seems to have been the pattern with Rodgers and Hammerstein, the first act of *Carousel* was in good shape, but the second was still in flux; the same had occurred with *Oklahoma!*, where act 2 was reworked significantly in Boston. Some of the changes in *Carousel* are clear from differences between the programs issued for the New Haven and Boston performances, at least in cases where decisions were made in time to influence the typesetting. On the first night in New Haven, *Carousel* ran way past midnight, and immediately after the curtain came down there was a two-hour production conference where cuts were hashed out (so Agnes de Mille said). Revisions were done quickly as the show moved from one place to the other, and also in Boston itself. The scene "up there" for Mr. and Mrs. God ("He" and "She" in the programs) was still in the show—Lawrence Langner found it "very gloomy indeed"—until Rodgers put his foot down and insisted on its replacement with Billy's less heretical encounter with the "Starkeeper" (see figure 3.3). This scene included "The Highest Judge of All" instead of having the song come just before, where it was moved to facilitate the change of set. The act 2 ballet still had a similar sequence to what was outlined in the January 1945 script, until it was cut down for being far too long (Langner refers to "the elimination of a maternity scene in the ballet, in which Julie gave birth to her child"). The different listing in the New Haven and Boston programs reveals that it also shifted from its position before

FIGURE 3.3 Billy Bigelow (John Raitt) and the Starkeeper (Russell Collins) in *Carousel* (1945). Photo by Eileen Darby/The LIFE Images Collection/Getty Images

the scene with Mr. and Mrs. God to after; we shall see the reason why in chapter 4. Finally, Langner took credit for suggesting Billy's reprise of "If I Loved You" in act 2, scene 5 (it is not listed in the Boston program, but it appears in the New York one): he says he then regretted it on dramatic grounds, but Rodgers refused to make another change given the remarkable impact it had on sheet-music sales of the song in the lobby of the Colonial Theatre.[18]

Reviews of the Boston *Carousel* were favorable. Elliot Norton, writing for the second time on it in the *Boston Post* (April 1, 1945), lauded "a new dramatic art form"; Elinor Hughes (*Boston Herald*, April 1) found it something "different from conventional musical comedy—a musical play, certainly; perhaps, even considering the nature of *Liliom*, a music drama," although she felt that it lacked cohesion, switched too abruptly between its various moods, and could not do justice to Molnár's nuanced dialogue (but neither could any musical play, she said). Like Norton, however, she thought the show much better on a second viewing after it had been tightened up, praising (on April 10) its "depth of feeling and emotional content." The anonymous reviewer in *Cue* (April 14) saw *Carousel* as "the beginning of our own authentic American opera," but added, "Call it what you like—young opera, musical play or tragedy—*Carousel* is another of the Guild's experiments, a new form of theatrical presentation with great future possibilities." The latter part of the Boston run was marred only by the death of President Roosevelt on April 12, 1945. But the New York newspapers were soon reporting on how Ferenc Molnár had expressed tearful approval of what had been done to his play. The dress rehearsal in the Majestic Theatre in New York may still have gone badly, so Langner said, but things looked bright for Broadway.[19]

## CHAPTER 4

# A DUET, A SOLILOQUY, AND A BALLET

THE SHOW RUNNING AT the Majestic Theatre just prior to *Carousel* was *Mexican Hayride* (it closed on March 17, 1945), with music and lyrics by Cole Porter and the book (spoken dialogue) by Herbert and Dorothy Fields. This was a showcase for the vaudeville star Bobby Clark and had a farrago of a plot involving a female bullfighter, a failed national lottery, and fugitives from Mexican justice adopting various imaginative disguises. It probably would not count as what scholars have labored to call the "integrated" musical, combining drama, music, and dance in a coherent way so as to create some higher-level unity. Certainly it could not compete in those terms with Rodgers and Hammerstein's *Oklahoma!* (1943), which is usually considered a watershed moment in the genre such that histories of American musical theater are often split into "before" and "after" phases. Here, Hammerstein gets credit for taking authorial control of both the book and the lyrics of his shows (as he had done before), and Rodgers, for writing songs to fit the drama. Agnes de Mille's choreography for *Oklahoma!*—and especially the dream ballet at the end of act 1—also gains significant recognition in this regard. But there were plenty of musicals before *Oklahoma!* that had a coherent plot from beginning to end and brought music and dance into the action rather than leaving them external to it.[1]

Therein lies the rub, however. Like opera, musical theater constantly struggles to deal with its *raison d'être*: that it is "musical." The issue is one of verisimilitude: if drama is meant to be somehow lifelike, then singing needs to be true to life, but it generally is not. There are conventional ways around the ensuing problems. For example, in the case of *Oklahoma!* one can plausibly sing and dance at a community gathering ("The Farmer and the Cowman") or a wedding (the song "Oklahoma"). Cowboys can also sing about a "beautiful mornin'," especially if, as with Curly, they are treated as Orpheus-like figures. In the absence of an excuse for songs that are realistic (or diegetic), there are other conventions available, such as the "I" song used to introduce a character (Ado Annie's "I Cain't Say No"), the narrative "let me tell you a story" one (Will Parker's "Kansas City"), or, in the case of duets, the "you" song as each character gives the other some instruction (Will and Ado Annie's "All er Nuthin'"). It also helps if the plot takes place in some faraway place veering into a fantasy world, or at least a pastoral one (Claremore, Oklahoma). As a last resort, one can claim that a song is somehow true to a no less real emotional life, plumbing depths that cannot be reached by words alone (Jud's "Lonely Room"). But that is a dangerous strategy.

Songs generally tend to freeze the plot in a shift from what is sometimes called "book time" to "lyric time."[2] In formal terms, lyric time tends to be circular given the role of musical repetition (this is true of opera arias as well). Thus one common song form—though it is not the only one—has a verse followed by a chorus (or refrain), the latter structured by way of four musical sentences of (often) eight measures each. These patterns determine the structure of the text, which will always be in some form of poetry (prose is for speech) with regular meter and rhyme. Rodgers and Hart's "This Can't Be Love" (from their *The Boys from Syracuse* of 1938) is a classic example (see example 4.1 ▶). The second section repeats the first, but with a full (closed) cadence rather than a half (open) one; the third contrasts with it in some kind of way as a "bridge" or "release" (also known as the "middle eight"); and the fourth returns in some way to the first with a more emphatic conclusion. Thus the form can be mapped as *AA′BA″* or *AA′BC*; four eight-measure periods produce a thirty-two-measure chorus, as in "This Can't Be Love," although in songs of this type the final section can be extended (e.g., 8 + 8 + 8 + 10 or 8 + 8 + 8 + 12). Other forms are also available, and in fact, not many Rodgers and Hammerstein songs fit the pattern exactly: even "People Will Say We're in Love" in *Oklahoma!*—in a regular *AA′BA″* form—doubles the phrase lengths.

Such repetitive structures do not allow for much dramatic action, although there can certainly be some rhetorical progression building to a final phrase that will often also fix the song's "hook" (a memorable line, sometimes also treated as the title of the song). "Action" songs would need to be handled carefully, anyway, because the

EXAMPLE 4.1 *The Boys from Syracuse* (1938), "This Can't Be Love," music by Richard Rodgers, lyrics by Lorenz Hart: (a) *A* section (mm. 17–24); (b) *B* section (mm. 32–40); (c) *A″* section (mm. 41–48)

audience's attention is elsewhere. Thus one could remove all the songs from *Oklahoma!* and it would still work as a coherent drama—as it did, of course, in Lynn Riggs's play—if not a very appealing one. The fact that the shift to lyric time also involves moving from one type of voice (speaking) to another (singing) creates other problems as well: Hammerstein talked about the difficulty of "oozing" from spoken dialogue to song.[3] Coming out of a song is easier: the audience's applause creates a rupture anyway. But continuing the dramatic action thereafter is not, given that the best response to applause is to leave the stage.

A songless *Oklahoma!* might seem absurd, but an equivalent *Carousel* is an impossibility. To that extent, Rodgers and Hammerstein's second show is far more "integrated" than their first. Of course, it adheres to at least some of the conventions outlined above. Happy seaside folks in Maine might plausibly sing of the delights of June, although why they should do the same for a clambake, "real nice" though it might be, is another matter. Rodgers and Hammerstein eventually decided to set up the inspiring anthem that consoles Julie Jordan on Billy Bigelow's death, "You'll Never Walk Alone," as a "real" song taught in school, and it is sung as such on its reprise at the end of the show.[4] As another convention, Carrie Pipperidge combines the "I" song with the narrative one when she predicts a rosy future "when I marry Mister Snow." She begins with a long verse ("His name is Mister Snow") leading to a chorus structured by way of the standard four-section pattern, though not in regular eight-measure groupings:

*A* ("When I marry Mister Snow"; 12 mm.; four lines of tetrameters)
*A* ("Then it's off to home we'll go"; 12 mm.; four tetrameters)
*B* ("He'll carry me 'cross the threshold"; 8 mm.; five trimeters)
*A′* ("Then I'll kiss him so he'll know"; 12 + 8 mm.; six tetrameters)

The *A* section starts with a lyrical phrase that can be adapted to end it; the *B* section is in a contrasted, more declamatory style (also to match the change in poetic meter); and the final *A′* section has an additional eight-measure coda built on a rising pattern to form an appropriate climax on the highest note of the song (see example 4.2 ▶). The fact

EXAMPLE 4.2 *Carousel*, "Mister Snow (Julie and Carrie Sequence)" (Carrie Pipperidge): (a) beginning of *A* section (mm. 113–16); (b) beginning of *B* section (mm. 137–40); (c) end of *A′* section (mm. 157–64)

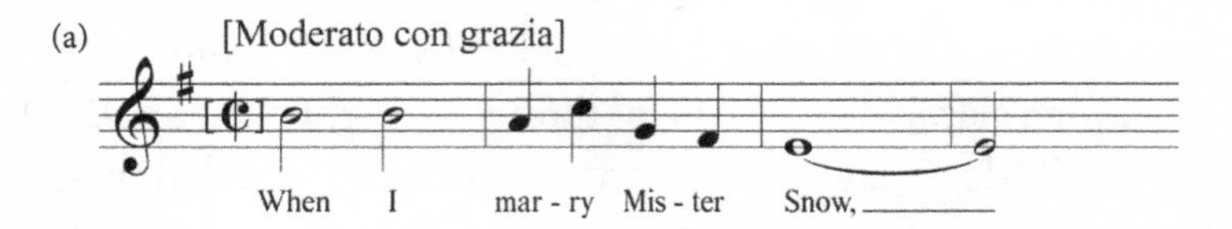

that the first two *A* sections are exactly the same—and are both "closed"—makes Carrie sound smug, which she is.

"Mister Snow" is as conventional as Carrie's dreams about marriage: it could easily be detached from its context, as it was for the purposes of sheet-music sales. But the song in fact comes at the end of a much longer musical sequence as Carrie starts out commenting on her friend's tendency to strangeness ("You're a queer one, Julie Jordan"), being "quieter and deeper than a well" and always getting distracted when sitting at her loom. "You're a queer one, Julie Jordan" and the following "His name is Mister Snow" both also start out as if they were themselves *AABA* forms, although they deviate, the former in the *B* section and the latter in the final *A* one. This is quite different from the songs in *Oklahoma!*—which are free-standing and relatively short, each tending to last around three minutes unless they are extended by dances. The "Julie and Carrie Sequence" in *Carousel* lasts more than five, and it is not even the longest musical part of this scene.

Even just the opening of *Carousel* is unusual. It follows Molnár's play as revised in German by Alfred Polgar in 1912 (followed in the 1921 New York version): instead of an overture before the curtain, we have a prologue (or "prelude," depending on which source one takes) that involves bustling stage action over the long "Carousel Waltz" (see figure 4.1). Rouben Mamoulian tended to like such pictorial openings: he used the technique for his staging of Dorothy and DuBose Heyward's *Porgy* for the Theatre Guild in 1927 (and in *Porgy and Bess* in 1935, which also included an "Occupational Humoresque" in act 3), as well as in the film *Love Me Tonight* (1932).[5] For the waltz, Rodgers drew

FIGURE 4.1 The opening scene of *Carousel* (1945). Courtesy of Rodgers & Hammerstein: An Imagem Company, www.rnh.com

in part on music he had written earlier in other circumstances, including material intended for but not used in the 1933 film *Hallelujah, I'm a Bum.*[6] But all these extended sequences give *Carousel* far more music than *Oklahoma!*—both in act 1 and still more in act 2, where, like many musicals, *Oklahoma!* tends to fall a bit flat. This greater musical emphasis onstage was also matched in the orchestra pit. The publicity leading up to *Carousel* emphasized that it would be scored for some forty players, including a full brass and woodwind section. This was in contrast to the twenty-eight for *Oklahoma!*—which already counted as large. Don Walker, who orchestrated the bulk of *Carousel* (along with Hans Spialek and others), worked with a rich palette. Rodgers was eager to make comparisons with the orchestra at the Metropolitan Opera, given that *Carousel* "came very close to opera," with "much that is operatic in the music." He might also have mentioned the same sized orchestra in Hammerstein's *Carmen Jones.*[7]

### THE "BENCH SCENE"

That "Julie and Carrie Sequence" comes after Julie's first encounter with Billy at the beginning of the act (following the prologue), which is done as speech given the presence of Mrs. Mullin. For their second meeting, however, Hammerstein planned in his scenario a scene that "drifts from dialogue into singing, eventually developing into a major refrain" with a song titled "The Wind Blows the Blossoms." Those blossoms came from the play, although Molnár handled the episode in a much briefer fashion, with no attempt to develop Julie and Liliom's relationship.

Hammerstein well knew that a musical *Liliom* needed something stronger. Billy has been fired from the carousel, and Julie has decided to stay out late with him, losing her job as well. The music previously heard at Carrie's "You're a queer one, Julie Jordan" (in G major) appears as underscoring to their dialogue (this is how Hammerstein "oozes") as Billy asks her name, which Julie sings at the appropriate point in the music. Billy whistles the answering phrase—he already had a tendency to whistle nonchalantly earlier in the scene—then restarts "You're a queer one" up a half step. Julie has new music as she tells Billy that she has no money for him to take; Billy again considers that she is "queer," up another half-step (he can be persuasive).[8] Julie repeats her "You couldn't take my money" music, explaining that she is "never goin' to marry." After more spoken dialogue over underscoring as Julie considers that she might in fact wed Billy "if I loved you," she repeats Carrie's earlier music and a variant of her words about working at the mill sitting distracted at the loom (which is what she would do if she loved Billy). Those repeated plugs of "if I loved you" are derived from the play: Julie's line "Yes, I would—if I loved you" was an addition to the 1921 English version (so, supplied by Lorenz Hart). But they set up the hook for the song: "If I Loved You" begins "warmly" (so the score is marked) in a luscious D-flat major.[9]

Julie's lyrical outburst leaves Billy somewhat nonplussed ("Well, anyway—you don't love me. That's what you said"). He finds distraction in the falling blossoms, but then discovers his own, surprisingly poetical voice to new music ("You can't hear a sound—not the turn of a leaf") as he wonders "what life is all about." Julie reckons that two heads are better than one "to figger it out." Billy turns poetical again

("There's a helluva lot o' stars in the sky"), realizing that two "little people" like them "don't count at all." Hammerstein also wrote a third stanza for the same music:

JULIE: There's a feathery little cloud floatin' by
Like a lonely leaf on a big blue stream.
BILLY: And two little people—you and I—
Who cares what we dream?

Rodgers set it to music (sixteen measures), but it was cut, with the music adapted (thirteen measures) to underscore Billy and Julie's spoken dialogue:[10] they have already started to match poetic rhymes, but they cannot yet sing in close musical agreement. Billy drops his reverie, suspicious that Julie is trying to maneuver him into marriage: he foresees himself "kinda scrawny and pale, pickin' at my food" (the music is the same as Julie's being distracted at the loom). He ends with the hook—he would wilt away "if I loved you," which gives the cue for Billy's repeat of the song. Rodgers ends it with a pause (for applause), though the scene is not over. There is more spoken dialogue over underscoring; the blossoms fall; and Billy and Julie kiss.

Stephen Sondheim called this scene "probably the single most important moment in the revolution of contemporary musicals."[11] That "revolution" lay in its complex fabric of spoken dialogue over underscoring, parlando declamation, lyric fragments akin to operatic arioso, and what one might as well call full-blown arias: all in all, an extraordinary twelve minutes or so of continuous music. Hammerstein rings the changes by moving between prose for the "spoken" dialogue (though some of it is sung) through a kind of free verse with irregular meter but clear rhymes ("If I Loved You") to stanzaic structures that are regular in both meter and rhyme ("You can't hear a sound"). He also designs the text to allow the sequence to combine musical ideas heard in a previous number—Carrie's "You're a queer one, Julie Jordan" and "When we work in the mill"—with those that are new. For Julie to repeat music previously sung to her by Carrie is plausible enough. But there are two oddities here. First, to have Julie sing her name at the beginning in time to the underscoring goes against the common pretense in musicals that characters are not musically self-aware: she should not be hearing what is going on in the orchestra. Billy's appropriation of Carrie's "You're a queer one" is even stranger: he was not onstage for the "Julie and Carrie Sequence," so he should not know either the melody or the words. However absurd the musical world might be, it needs to have its own internal logic. But here that logic seems overruled by the dramatic and musical ambitions for the scene, with its echoes, statements, and foretellings ("Soon you'd leave me, / Off you would go in the mist of day").

All that came slowly in the drafting process. Hammerstein said in 1951 that in the case of "If I Loved You," "the melody—the entire melody—was written first, and I set the lyric to it." However, a first version of the words suggests a more complicated process, with some of the musical elements in place but not others:[12]

BILLY: Ah . . . How do you know what you'd do if you loved me? Or how you'd feel . . . or anythin'?

JULIE: I dunno how I know.

BILLY: Ah.

JULIE: Sometimes you know things that y' can't say so good why ya know 'em but you do.

If I loved you
I would tremble ev'ry time you'd say my name,
But I'd long to hear you say it just the same.
I dunno jest how I know, but I ken see
How everythin' would be.
If I loved you . . .
If I loved you
I'd be too a-skeered t' say what's in my heart
I'd be too a-skeered to even make a start
And my golden chance to speak would come and go
And you would never know
How I loved you—
If I loved you.

The hook ("If I loved you") is already clear, and by this point at least some of the music for the song itself had been composed: the two lines for the *B* section (rhyming "heart" and "start") fit, although the "a-skeered" repetition is awkward. These lines then lead back into some version of the familiar *A* section to end in the same way as the final version (although Hammerstein's "golden chance" gets taken back into the *B* section as "golden chances"). The apparent beginning of the song is not at all well formed, however. The second and third lines ("I would tremble") are in the wrong poetic meter: they were eventually replaced by Julie's statement, before the song proper, of how she would work distractedly at the loom if she loved Billy (therefore allowing the repetition of prior musical material). Rodgers and Hammerstein also realized that

"If I Loved You" itself should begin after, rather than before, Julie realizes that she "ken see / How everythin' would be." Thus they adapted it for the lead-in ("But somehow I ken see / Jest exackly how I'd be")—creating a rather awkward modulation in the process—and had to come up with new lines for the initial *A* sections ("If I loved you, / Time and again I would try to say"). This seems to have been typical of how they worked: rather than Rodgers setting a pre-formed lyric or Hammerstein putting words to pre-composed music, they each came up with fragmentary ideas (musical or textual) that then fed one off the other.

Treating what Julie "ken see" as the cue for "If I Loved You" turns the song into a fantasy number about the future, which helps justify the lyrical moment just as in the case of Carrie's "Mister Snow." But there were also other issues to be resolved here. Hammerstein wrote in 1949 about the problem (which seemed "insurmountable") of writing an initial love duet for Curly and Laurey in *Oklahoma!* given that they are clearly in love but not yet ready to admit it.[13] His solution was a song full of negative imperatives—"Don't!" (throw bouquets at me, hold my hand too much, etc.)—lest "People Will Say We're in Love." His point was that while he needed to secure the relationship between the lead roles, too early an open declaration of love meant that there would be little left for the forthcoming drama to achieve. He had already tried a different solution to the problem in *Show Boat* with Ravenal and Magnolia's duet at their first encounter, "Make Believe" (the characters agree to imagine, for the moment, that "I love you"). "If I Loved You" works in a similar way: the conditional "if" in its opening line, already negated by both Julie and Billy in a spoken interjection ("But you don't"), opens up a space for their coming together. However, "People Will Say We're in Love" and "Make Believe" are both "you" songs: they start with imperatives as one character tells the other what or what not to do. "If I Loved You," on the other hand, tends to stay in "I" mode (the "you"s are mostly object pronouns): Billy and Julie mostly sing at, rather than to, each other.

Carrie and Enoch Snow have an easier time of it in their own "Sequence" later in act 1, where they engage with each other and harmonize together (in "When the Children Are Asleep"); their music is also much simpler. But in "If I Loved You" there is a curious lack of interaction between Billy and Julie: curt answers, prolonged silences, and constant distractions (those falling blossoms). Even Billy's statement of the main theme seems sung to himself: an earlier draft preceded it with "And I know I would be / Like you said you'd be with me."[14] This is followed in the sheet music, but we lose that "you" moment in the final version: Billy reverts to Julie's "But somehow I can see" (expressed in more standard English, which suggests a very late editorial insertion). This is clear also in what little evidence we have of the original production by way of Jan Clayton and John Raitt's re-creation of the scene for the televised *General Foods 25th Anniversary Show: A Salute to Rodgers and Hammerstein* (1954): despite the close camera work (because of the medium), the staging of the main song tends to leave the characters on their own. Inevitably, music grants them greater articulacy: they can sing about what they are "afraid and shy" to reveal. However, the "if" does not bode well.

One can easily read the differences between those first and final versions of the text of "If I Loved You" as a search for greater dramatic effect. But Rodgers and Hammerstein also had another agenda. Whatever their musical ambitions for *Carousel*, they still needed to market its main songs by way of sheet music or the radio: this was a standard, and very profitable, part of the business of musical theater. Thus "If I Loved You" becomes a straightforward *AABA* song with two eight-measure sections (*AA′*, each with three short lines of text), a third for the *B* section ("Longin' to tell you" as two elegant pentameters), and then a return to *A″* that stretches to twelve measures (five lines) by way of a cunning enjambment ("Never, never to know / How I loved you— / If I loved you"). Such marketing was aided by the reprise of the number late in act 2 as Billy sees Julie during his day on earth (the song now ends "And you never will know / How I loved you, / How I loved you"). That reprise was added during the Boston tryout, though it now seems inevitable as a way of resolving the hanging "if" that has left its gloomy shadow over the show thus far. At its first appearance, the song ends with a kiss. But in the very next scene—as June busts out all over—Julie is Mrs. Bigelow and has to admit to Carrie that her marriage is in deep trouble: "Last Monday he hit me."

### *"SOLILOQUY"*

Part of the power of the "Bench scene" lies in its giving voice to two characters who otherwise seem emotionally stunted, as they certainly are in Molnár's treatment of them. Here Hammerstein also grants Billy something that the play does not—a chance "to wonder what life is all about"—and the music gives him still greater lyric intensity. It makes us inclined to sympathize with him, though whether we should is another matter.

This is a typical problem of musical theater: a character who sings so well cannot be all bad. Molnár's Liliom is drawn narrowly, but Rodgers and Hammerstein flesh him out. This is clear, too, in their handling of the moment that convinced them to take on the play in the first place. Liliom reacts somewhat coolly to Julie's news that she is pregnant; he has unfinished business with Ficsúr and Mrs. Muskat (as does Billy with Jigger Craigin and Mrs. Mullin), and the news only sinks in when he is left alone. Molnár handled it in a few short lines at the very end of his second scene:

> LILIOM: Aunt Hollunder! (*With naïve joy.*) Julie's going to have a baby. (*Then he goes to the window, jumps on the sofa, looks out. Suddenly, in a voice that overtops the droning of the organ, he shouts as if addressing the far-off carousel.*) I'm going to be a father.

Julie enters to ask "What's happened?" Liliom reverts to type: "Nothing," he replies, burying his face in a cushion. Julie covers him with a shawl; she stands at the door listening to the organ; and the curtain falls.

At their first production meeting in early December 1943, Rodgers already had the idea of a more substantial number for Billy's excitement at the prospect of being a father to a son, then realizing that it might be a daughter instead (an experience with which the composer himself was familiar). It took a while to bring that to fruition, however. Rodgers later described the process:

> When we began discussing the "Soliloquy" well before either of us did any writing, I asked Oscar, "How would this be for the

music?" At the piano I gave him an idea—not the actual melody, but the general tone, color and emotion I thought would be appropriate. I know this helped him when he wrote the words, and it certainly helped me when I wrote the music.

He also said that it took Hammerstein two weeks to write the text, though typically the music came quickly (in two hours, according to Agnes de Mille).[15] As with "If I Loved You," fantasy frees up a musical space that is defined here by two fairly regular songs: "My boy, Bill!" and "My little girl" (see example 4.3 ▶). But they are sandwiched between extensive sections that defy such easy classification, with music

EXAMPLE 4.3 *Carousel*, "Soliloquy" (Billy Bigelow): (a) mm. 42–48 ("My boy, Bill!"); (b) mm. 222–25 ("My little girl")

ranging from monotone declamation to melodic passages that might themselves seem like "songs" if only they had the proper form. The closest precedent for this, significantly enough, is Jud's "Lonely Room" in *Oklahoma!*, and there are other echoes here as well, we shall see. But again there is a massive increase in scale: in their original-cast recordings, "Lonely Room" lasts for 2′36″ and "Soliloquy," 7′30″.

Hammerstein's printed libretto gives the text as a succession of short lines, but for the most part it falls into regular four-line stanzas:

> I wonder what he'll think of me!
> I guess he'll call me "The old man."
> I guess he'll think I can lick
> Ev'ry other feller's father—Well, I can!
>
> I bet that he'll turn out to be
> The spit an' image of his dad.
> But he'll have more common sense
> Than his puddin'-headed father ever had.

This is well crafted in terms of the rhymes across stanzas ("me . . . be") and within them ("man . . . can," "dad . . . had"), plus the enjambment between the (unrhymed) third and fourth lines. The stanzas allow for strophic setting (the same music for each one); the rhymes enable parallel musical phrases; and the enjambment drives through two lines to the cadence.

Three stanzas serve as the "verse"—although one wonders if that is the right term—to the chorus, "My boy, Bill!" This starts out as if it will be in the standard thirty-two measures, with two *A* sections, then a *B* one ("Like a tree he'll grow"). However, the *B* section lasts sixteen measures rather than eight, and its ending is interrupted by an interjection that comes one measure too soon ("No . . . "). This marks a change of direction: instead of some return to *A*, the music continues differently (". . . pot-bellied, baggy-eyed bully'll boss him around!"). Hammerstein has prompted that by his change of meter ("No pot-bellied . . . around" is a pentameter), but it was also convenient, for the lack of a return forces the number to continue. The text moves back to four-line stanzas as Billy thinks more about his son's likely occupations ("I don't give a damn what he does"): Rodgers sets all four stanzas to simple declamation. Even the son's becoming president of the United States would be "all right, too." The orchestra starts a repeat of "My boy, Bill!" while Billy speaks ("His mother 'd like that") before picking up the melody at the end of the first *A* section ("Not Bill!") and continuing through the second *A* into the *B* section. This again leads to an extension for "No flat-bottomed, flabby-faced, pot-bellied, baggy-eyed bastard'll boss him around!"—Hammerstein's pentameter has become longer still. The text returns to four-line stanzas ("And I'm damned if he'll marry the boss's daughter")—more declamation—until Billy wonders (in a prose-like interjection) why he is so worried: "My kid ain't even been born yet!" He then resumes his fantasy at "I can see him / When he's seventeen or so / And startin' in to go / With a girl"). This begins as if it were to be the first two *A* sections of a song, but instead of the *B* one, Billy returns to prose ("Wait a minute!") as he suddenly realizes that his "son" could be a daughter.

Billy goes back to where he started. His "She mightn't be so bad at that" has the same music as at the beginning ("I wonder what he'll think of me!"). A daughter is a very different proposition, however, and the following song, "My little girl," is far less rambunctious than "My boy, Bill!" It is also more clearly rounded in a straightforward *AA′BA″* form (4 + 4 + 8 + 8 mm.).[16] But again there is a disruption. In a quite extraordinary coda, Billy suddenly panics:

I got to get ready before she comes!
I got to make certain that she
Won't be dragged up in slums
With a lot o' bums—
Like me!

Hammerstein had made a similar poetic shift, and to the same meter, at the climax of Jud's "Lonely Room" in *Oklahoma!*

I ain't gonna dream 'bout her arms no more!
I ain't gonna leave her alone!
Goin' outside,
Git myself a bride,
Git me a womern to call my own.

Rodgers also makes the parallel clear by way of a very similar musical setting (see example 4.4 ▶).[17] Jud and Billy are both outsiders to the community; they are each also dysfunctional within it, and they are killed by their own knives. Billy, however, will be offered some manner of redemption.

EXAMPLE 4.4 (a) *Carousel*, "Soliloquy," mm. 248–52; (b) *Oklahoma!*, "Lonely Room" (Jud Fry), mm. 44–47

"Soliloquy" anticipates Billy's death: the final lines concern his need for money—"I'll go out and make it / Or steal it or take it / Or die!" Hammerstein was anxious to establish some—any—justification for Billy's decision to turn to crime. Molnár spends little time on his motivation: Liliom just has the vague plan to take Julie and the baby to America. "Soliloquy" makes things clearer: Billy needs to provide for

EXAMPLE 4.4 Continued

his imagined daughter. That probably does not excuse his actions. But Rodgers and Hammerstein seem to have considered it an extenuating circumstance.

## "LOUISE'S BALLET"

The main dances in *Carousel* come at the end of "June Is Bustin' Out All Over" ("Girls' Dance"), in the "Hornpipe" at the end of "Blow High, Blow Low" (mostly for the men, but also with a *pas de deux*), and in the act 2 ballet; another dance at the end of "A Real Nice Clambake" was cut during the Boston tryout. They were the responsibility of the choreographer, Agnes de Mille, who also tried to take a late hand in the staging of the "Carousel Waltz" in the prologue. The dances following the songs were conventional enough. De Mille later said, however, that the ballet was "probably the hardest challenge" she had ever met: "It entailed a real job of dramatic invention, close to playwrighting." This was no doubt because of narrative issues (with new characters and action) and also musical ones (finding appropriate songs to match).[18]

Billy's realization in "Soliloquy" that he might have a daughter establishes in ways better than the play what will happen later in act 2 during his trial "in the beyond" as he is given his chance for a day back on earth. Molnár's Liliom is urged by the Magistrate to do "some good deed" for her, but without any explanation of why she needs it, and in the final scene of the play, Louise seems perfectly content with her life alongside her widowed mother: all she knows is that her father went to America and died there. The Starkeeper in *Carousel* makes a different case, however. As he reveals to Billy that Julie has had a daughter, who is now fifteen years old, Billy asks if she is "happy." "No, she ain't," the Starkeeper replies: "She's a lot like you. That's why I figure you're the one could help her most—if you was there."

Thus it becomes the role of the act 2 ballet both to introduce Louise and to explain what "help" she needs. In Hammerstein's draft scenario, the ballet has a different position as well as content. Using "reprises and new music" it would represent Billy's ascent "up there" on his death, then cover events of the next "seventeen" years: the baby is born, Ficsúr is hanged, Wolf and Marie get richer and have children, Dwight and the Carpenter appear, and Louise becomes a young woman. This covers a staging problem (how to get Billy "up there") and also ties up some loose ends left hanging in the play (what happens to Ficsúr or the Carpenter) and in the scenario (Dwight). Its position was also a result of the location of the separate scenes in the act. As a practical matter, any scene requiring a full-stage set (as the ballet would) needs to be bounded on either side by scenes done "in one" or on some kind of half-stage set so as to allow the full-stage one to be prepared out of sight of the audience. The scenario follows the play: Billy is brought from the scene of the crime (the culvert) to what Hammerstein knew would "probably" be some interior set for his last words with Julie. Then immediately after the ballet comes the scene with Mr. and Mrs. God in their "front parlor," then the one in Louise's bedroom. That bedroom scene in turn allows the full-stage set to be switched to the final one for the schoolhouse lawn.

This is how the sequence played out in the New Haven tryout according to its program (Billy dies in his and Julie's "room"). But it had already been decided to have Billy stay fallen at the scene of the crime (the "mainland waterfront"), combining two scenes into one. Hammerstein credited Molnár with suggesting this when he attended a rehearsal of *Carousel*, and the shift was made in time for it to be included in the program printed for Boston.[19] As a result, the ballet was moved after the scene with Mr. and Mrs. God (so on a full-stage set prepared during that scene and changed during the subsequent one outside Julie's cottage), and Billy's "The Highest Judge of All" was taken back to cover the transition from "down here" to "up there."

The New Haven version of the ballet was already simpler than what Hammerstein had originally imagined in his scenario. The program called it an "Interlude" ("Billy Makes a Journey") and divided it into two parts labeled A ("The Birth of Billy's Child") and B ("The Childhood"). Although section B would seem to suggest some passing of time (and so a review of events over however many years), the list of performers shows that it was close to the final version, with a younger Miss Snow, five brothers and sisters Snow, two badly brought up boys, a young man like Billy, a carnival woman, and ten members of the carnival troupe. Section A was dropped for Boston, and the title "Interlude" was changed to "Ballet," though the list of characters stays the same, as it does in the New York program. Thus the Boston audience saw something close to the final version of the ballet: Louise romps on the beach in tomboy fashion with two ruffian-like boys; she is snubbed by the Snow children and insulted by one of the daughters ("Your father was a thief"); a carnival troupe enters, and its leader (who looks like Billy when he was young) flirts with her but then leaves; and a group of children (unidentified in the libretto, but presumably the Snows) enter dressed for a party and rebuff Louise's attempt to join them, leading her to cry out, "I hate you—I hate all of you!" She is left "heartbroken and alone—terribly alone." It is not clear how much time is meant to have passed during the ballet, but its four distinct episodes could come close enough together. However, there remained some confusion over the Snow children. There are six in the ballet, but Carrie says in the next scene that she has nine, and the young actor (Ralph

Linn, Bambi's younger brother) who played Enoch Snow Jr. in that scene was one of the "two little ruffian boys" in the ballet.

Hammerstein developed his ideas on the ballet as he moved from the scenario to drafting the libretto (where he wanted a "union of ballet, opera, drama, and pantomime"), and Agnes de Mille worked still more of it out in her own planning and then with her dancers in rehearsal. She also knew to take with a grain of salt Hammerstein's preference (in the scenario) for "singing, dialogue, pantomime, and dancing." He had originally wanted some similar combination for the extended ballet at the end of act 1 of *Oklahoma!*—he was suspicious of the narrative potential of dance on its own—although de Mille managed to elaborate his idea of Laurey's "dream" without resorting to dialogue. But a dream was one thing and real life another, and "Louise's Ballet" needed at least some spoken dialogue in order to make clear what Billy had to do.[20]

The music was worked out in rehearsal as well, if on the basis of a limited set of choices. In *Oklahoma!* de Mille had been able to string together songs heard earlier in act 1 that linked (quite neatly, in fact) to events or characters in Laurey's dream ("Oh, What a Beautiful Mornin'" for her wedding, "I Cain't Say No" for Jud's "postcard girls," and so on): only in a few places did the orchestrator, Robert Russell Bennett, need to come up with additional music on the fly (because Rodgers did not regard it as his responsibility). "Louise's Ballet" in *Carousel* was more problematic because it introduced entirely new characters rather than fantasy versions of those already seen. De Mille relied on her accompanist, Trude Rittman (Rittmann), who had been working with American dancers since her arrival in the United States in 1937 (she fled Nazi Germany in 1933). Rittman was a gifted composer in her own right, and she had already provided the musical arrangements for de Mille's choreography in Kurt Weill's *One Touch of Venus* (1943) and Harold Arlen's *Bloomer Girl* (1944). Following her work on *Carousel*, she retained close ties with Rodgers and Hammerstein, providing arrangements and even original music for their *South Pacific*, *The King and I*, and *The Sound of Music*.[21]

Despite the new characters and situations, Rittman was able to find some music from earlier in *Carousel* that made thematic sense, such as part of the opening of "When the Children Are Asleep" for the Snow children. Likewise, for the carnival troupe she used the "Carousel Waltz" (which in the ballet is given the strange tempo indication "Tempo di Valse Banal"—presumably an in-joke not in fact intended for public consumption). Some of Rittman's other choices set up poignant references. For example, the ballet begins with Louise dancing alone to "If I Loved You." The more predictable option, "My little girl" from "Soliloquy," was cued by Billy's final remark to the Starkeeper as he catches sight of Louise, but it might not have seemed strong enough as an opening gesture, and "If I Loved You" also presents an issue that Billy will need to resolve. Similarly, Louise's encounter with the leader of the carnival troupe is paired with "I wonder what he'll think of me" from "Soliloquy," then leading to "My boy, Bill!" The latter resonates for Billy and also, in some sense, for Louise, who is attracted to a younger version of the father she has never known. Elsewhere, the musical source seems purely utilitarian: Louise's dance with the two young ruffians is done to music heard toward the beginning of "June Is Bustin' Out All Over" (at "You'll get no drinks er vittles"); the extended "polonaise" for the children's party from which Louise is excluded is a cunning adaptation of music from "When the Children Are Asleep" (see example 4.5 ▶); and even some seemingly independent linking passages can be related to previous material.

EXAMPLE 4.5 (a) *Carousel*, "Louise's Ballet," mm. 436–39; (b) "When the Children Are Asleep" (Enoch Snow), mm. 5–8

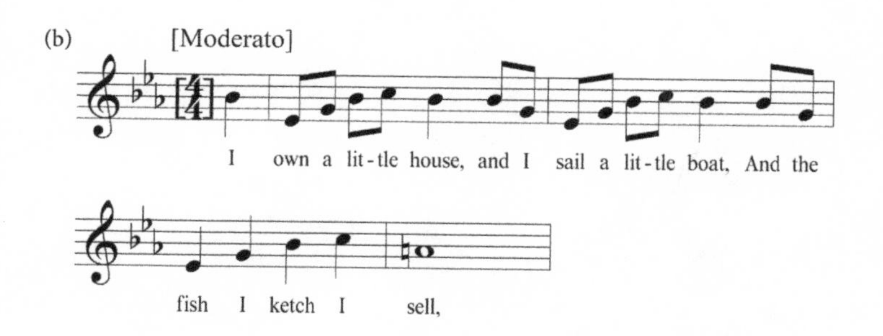


At the ballet's end, we move to underscoring for Billy and the Starkeeper's final spoken exchange, done to what we have long expected: "My little girl." Billy is moved by Louise's plight—"Somebody ought to help her," he says—and the Starkeeper repeats the offer for Billy to "go down any time." In the play, Liliom has no choice in the matter. For Billy, however, his task is now clear.

**CHAPTER 5**

# THE PROBLEMS OF AN ENDING

MOLNÁR'S *LILIOM* WAS ABOUT "the life and death of a scoundrel" according to its Hungarian subtitle, which took on additional meaning in light of his personal circumstances at the time of writing the play given that his own marriage to Margit Vészi was breaking down; they divorced in 1910, when their daughter was three years old.[1] The play was also called a "suburban legend" in both its Hungarian and German versions, which creates a disconnect between the prosaic and the mythical. Thus the play is clear on the location of the action (the working-class outskirts of Budapest), though that could shift easily enough to any other (sub)urban environment: the production in Vienna in 1913 situated it in the Wurstelprater. But there is no indication of the period or date (save a generic "spring"), which could well be any time in the later nineteenth or early twentieth centuries, or, for that matter, whenever the play happens to be performed.

Rodgers and Hammerstein locate *Carousel* in anything but a specific urban or suburban context: their "New England coast" is much vaguer. However, they situate the action in a precise fifteen-year period between 1873 and 1888. It had served a purpose to set *Oklahoma!* "just after the turn of the century," before Oklahoma became a state in 1907. There is no obvious reason for these dates for *Carousel*, however, other than just putting it in some specific "other" time. Distancing the characters in this way allowed some kind of detachment from their moral ambiguities: Billy and Julie live "then," not "now." It also, typically, provided a further justification for entering the other world of song: not until their *Me and Juliet* (1953) did Rodgers and Hammerstein attempt to write a show set directly in the present, and here they justified it by way of the typical formula of the "backstage musical" (a show about putting on a show). But while *Carousel* is firmly located in a "then," its messages seem clearly directed to the "now" of 1945.

Hammerstein was not afraid of dealing with social issues: *Show Boat* engages with race and miscegenation, and it features a reprobate, Gaylord Ravenal, as its leading man. Rodgers and Hart had also exploited an unsavory antihero, fired from his job as an entertainer, in their *Pal Joey* (1940). Billy Bigelow, however, is less debonair than either Ravenal or Joey Evans, and less prone to being construed as a "lovable rogue" for all that some productions of *Carousel* seek to cast him that light. As we have seen, his music lures us into sympathy, but it is a dangerous seduction. *Oklahoma!*

had already opened this can of worms in the case of Jud Fry; some had advocated dropping the character from its source play (*Green Grow the Lilacs*), though Hammerstein said that he was the "bass fiddle" that brought depth to an otherwise anodyne plot concerning the wholly predictable lives of cowboys and farmers. But Jud's tendency to violence could just about be contained within the frontier environment, and, failing all else, his death at the end of the show solved most of the problems that remained; certainly it has no impact on Curly and Laurey's happy-ever-after future.[2]

In *Carousel*, however, Jud comes back to life in the form of Billy Bigelow, another outsider prone to violence, but one now front and center in the drama. Julie Jordan also suffers the consequences of his actions in a real world quite distant from Laurey's dream-ballet nightmares about Jud. Julie is represented as strong-willed and independent: she has gone out with other men and is "never goin' to marry," she says (though she does). Hammerstein seems to have worried about the consequences, eventually removing from *Liliom* the dilemma posed by the Carpenter (he is mentioned briefly in the scenario in connection with the act 2 ballet), who is the safe option that Molnár's Julie repeatedly refuses. Laurey appears no less hard-headed at the start of *Oklahoma!*—it was required of wartime women—but, inevitably, she softens in the end. Julie has a different outcome, however, and some might consider her foolish for staying with Billy through thick and thin.

Matters came to a head regarding how to escape what Hammerstein called the "tunnel" of the play's last scenes with Liliom's death and its aftermath.[3] Liliom teams up with Ficsúr to steal money that will enable him to take Julie to

America; Billy's ambition is to go to San Francisco (New York in Hammerstein's scenario). The robbery goes bad, and, faced with his arrest, Billy (like Liliom) stabs himself. We might wish to argue over the nobility of that desperate act or of Billy's motives for turning to crime in the first place. But they made Hammerstein uncomfortable; he cut down drastically Liliom's deathbed admission to Julie of his hopes and failures, and he likewise simplified the process of his judgment by the Starkeeper, who seems more good-natured than Molnár's stern magistrate. Rodgers and Hammerstein probably did not want to engage with the theological problems posed by any "crimson fire": fifteen years pass by in a flash (as the Starkeeper says, "A year on earth is just a minute up here"). But they had fewer choices when it came to handling the action during Billy's day back on earth and the failed encounter with his (now teenage) daughter, Louise. The only question that remained was whether Billy could still gain admission through the back door of heaven.

Molnár strongly implies that the consequence of Liliom's ill-treatment of Louise is eternal punishment: as the two Heavenly Policemen follow him off, the first "makes a deploring gesture," and both "shake their heads deploringly." We are left with a final enigmatic exchange between mother and daughter that was added in the 1912 German version of the play and hence entered the 1921 English translation. Louise asks, "Is it possible for someone to hit you—hard like that—real loud and hard—and not hurt you at all?" "It is possible, dear," Julie replies, "that someone may beat you and beat you and beat you—and not hurt you at all." It may have seemed attractive to leave any reading of

Liliom's fate to a "deploring gesture." But Louise and Julie's last two lines provided much food for thought.

In a long discussion of the 1921 New York production, drama critic Burns Mantle found cause to gripe:

> The Molnar *Liliom* is a curious blend of fact and fantasy, muddled as to its theme and rather vague in its conclusions; one of those imaginative affairs into which you, as auditor, are privileged to read your own meanings. It is the sort of play that flatters the so-classified intelligent public to which the Theater Guild frankly appeals, and is guaranteed a certain popularity with the larger and less easily influenced public by reason of the attractiveness of its production. . . . Personally, we have little patience with the drama that has to be explained, counting the effort of the playwright and producer as of negative value if their play does not explain itself. But we would not deny the intellectuals the joy they will extract from *Liliom*.[4]

Such "joy" extended to some amusing debate in other newspapers of the time about whether Liliom ends up in heaven or hell (the tendency was to assume the former). In 1940, however, Brooks Atkinson, the eminent theater critic of the *New York Times*, came up with a different, somewhat perverse reading of the dilemmas posed by *Liliom* when writing his review of the current staging of "one of the most beautiful plays in the modern theatre." He also returned to them in a subsequent think piece: Liliom is a "romantic hero," and while some might object to this "braggart and bully," one needs to ask what makes him so "endearing and poignant" and "one of the most captivating figures in the modern drama," depicted "fondly and humorously" by Molnár. The answer, Atkinson suggests, lies both in Liliom's "charm" and in the fact that he is "a great lover." Julie, too, gains Atkinson's approval, for "it is proof of her independence of mind and of Liliom's richness of spirit that she loves him, endures all his waywardness and remains true to his memory long after his death." For Atkinson, Liliom's refusal to repent at the end, condemning himself to "eternal punishment," is a sign almost of nobility: "Love makes Liliom a desperate man. He cannot yield to it without surrendering himself, and he cannot surrender himself in heaven."[5]

### UP OR DOWN?

Ennobling Billy as if he were a Don Juan is no less troublesome than treating him as a lovable rogue. But each of the three film treatments of *Liliom* had to come up with a clearer outcome. The 1921 *A Trip to Paradise* avoided most of the problems by way of a trick also adopted in the screen version of *Cabin in the Sky* (1943): the Liliom character is only left unconscious after his crime—with a relatively good deed to his credit—and when he recovers, he is a changed man. The 1930 film, however, sticks more closely to the play throughout. Liliom is brought up from the "crimson fire" on an iron-clad train. He transfers to a more elegant carriage where he once more encounters the Chief Magistrate, alongside the angel Gabriel bearing a shell-like horn. The magistrate allows Liliom to see Louise outside Julie's cottage, and with similar results to those in the play (but he tries to give her the horn rather than a star, and he slaps her across the cheek). Louise calls for her mother, and Liliom, standing back on the train, laments his failure. But the magistrate says, "No, Liliom, you have not failed," and tells him to listen. We then get the "not hurt you at all" exchange between Julie and Louise. Liliom asks for another chance, but the magistrate gently refuses: "You'd only spoil it. The memory of you makes them much happier than ever you could make them" (cue hymn-like underscoring). Liliom accepts the argument, taking some pride in Louise having described her father as handsome, and in Julie still turning down the Carpenter. The magistrate responds sententiously: "Women like Julie are endlessly faithful. It's touching; it's mysterious." He leads Liliom off, and the final shot (the hymn changes to an ascending solo violin) shows the train wending its way up a viaduct to heaven.

The 1934 French film, directed by Fritz Lang, avoids this troublesome appeal to the eternal feminine. The Heavenly Magistrate (Le Commissaire) interviews Liliom in his office and shows him film footage (stored in heaven) of one violent episode between Liliom and Julie that we have already seen, but now with a different soundtrack—not Liliom's words but his thoughts (his frustration at his inability to articulate his real feelings or to correct his behavior). For Liliom's return to earth, a scale is set up in heaven to weigh his actions. When he disabuses Louise of the rather rosy picture she has of her long-dead father, a rather whimsically presented devil places heavy weights on the negative side of the scale. However, Liliom's guardian angel picks up the star Louise has refused and puts it on the plus side. Liliom has a second encounter with his daughter, but she rejects his approach, leading him to slap her (more weights added by the devil). Back in heaven, the magistrate accuses Liliom of being incorrigible, but his and Liliom's attention is suddenly caught (thanks to the office's beautiful secretary, whom Liliom has already charmed) by Julie and Louise's "not hurt you at all" exchange. A tear falls down Liliom's cheek; the scales tip the other way; and the final shot reveals a starry sky above a heavenly chorus both seen and heard.

Lang's ending to *Liliom* is theologically suspect, at best, and the film was roundly condemned by the French Catholic clergy.[6] But there were also other issues in play. The 1930 Julie does not see Liliom; the 1934 one glimpses him briefly through a window but treats it as a figment of her imagination. Both films seem to have been anxious over the part of the play where Julie and Liliom meet on his day back on earth (she thinks he is a beggar) and the implausibility of her not recognizing him. It hardly matters anyway, for the main focus is on Liliom's treatment of Louise. Given the conventions of a Broadway musical, however, *Carousel* could not afford to leave the lead couple in such an unresolved state.

In his act 2, scene 5, Hammerstein revises and extends the play's exchange between Julie and Marie, in part to establish the upcoming graduation ceremony. Carrie tells of her recent trip to New York, singing a snatch of a song ("I'm a Tomboy") from a risqué show she saw there. Enoch Snow enters with his eldest son and catches her in the act. Julie goes into the house as Carrie and Enoch exit. What happens next, as Billy enters with the Heavenly Friend, is entirely new. As they watch from the side, Louise confesses to Enoch Jr. that she is planning to run away to join a theater troupe (building on what had already been enacted in "Louise's Ballet"). Enoch Jr. wants her to stay and will marry her to make it happen, but he fumbles the proposal out of fear of paternal disapproval, causing Louise to chase him off, then fall sobbing. This gives Billy the excuse he needs to make himself appear to her.

Their subsequent dialogue rearranges elements of the play but is close enough to it in substance, including Louise's rejection of the star and the slap on the hand. She calls for her mother, leading to a slightly toned down but still troublesome version of the "not hurt you at all" exchange: Julie refers to being "hit"—and "hard"—but does not have the "beat you and beat you and beat you" repetition. This is not the end of the matter, however. Louise goes into the house; Julie sees the star that Billy has left on a chair, picks it up, and holds it to her breast, standing silently while Billy sings his reprise of "If I Loved You." The lights fade as Julie goes inside, and Billy comments to the Heavenly Friend that Julie seemed to know he was there. "Julie would always know," says the Heavenly Friend, and the two agree that she "never changes." Billy then realizes that he still needs to do something for Louise and demands to see her graduation (see figure 5.1).

The way is now clear for Billy to do some further redemptive act—something denied him in all prior treatments of the story. As Dr. Seldon, the local doctor, gives the commencement address, Billy notices his resemblance to the Starkeeper. The doctor urges the graduating students to find their own way to happiness and not to let the failures of their parents hold them back: Billy whispers words of encouragement to Louise ("Listen to him. Believe him"). The students follow the doctor's cue to sing the school song (a reprise of "You'll Never Walk Alone"), and at the second line ("And don't be afraid of the dark") he speaks to her again ("Believe him, darling! Believe"). As the music continues,

FIGURE 5.1 The graduation scene at the end of *Carousel* (1945). Courtesy of Rodgers & Hammerstein: An Imagem Company, www.rnh.com

he crosses over to his wife—"I loved you, Julie. Know that I loved you!"—inspiring her to add her own voice to the throng. Thus there is no need for any "deploring gesture." The Heavenly Friend "smiles," the doctor-cum-Starkeeper "smiles wisely," and as Billy is led off, the ensemble affirms "You'll never walk alone" in rousing six-part harmony.

Dr. Seldon is listed as a "minister" in the New Haven and Boston programs (he is not mentioned in the New York one), played by Russell Collins, who was Mr. God in New Haven and Boston and the Starkeeper on Broadway (Mrs. God disappeared from the cast). The idea of doubling a character "up there" and "down here" had already been adopted by Fritz Lang (Le Commissaire appeared as a police commissioner in an earlier, invented scene), and it was also adopted in the film version of *Cabin in the Sky*. But Hammerstein could just as well have taken it from another film dealing with a fantasy world somewhere over the rainbow, *The Wizard of Oz* (1939). In contrast to all previous treatments of *Liliom*, however, Hammerstein's kindly Starkeeper seems well disposed to Billy right from the start. Billy certainly needs to do something to gain redemption; Julie's love is not enough on its own. It does not take much, however: just a gentle, encouraging word here and there seems to make his future assured. It is hard nowadays to let him off so lightly.

### A POSTWAR MESSAGE

The inspirational tone of "You'll Never Walk Alone" in April 1945 was as much a case of wartime propaganda as praising the land that is "grand" in *Oklahoma!* in March 1943.

Hammerstein went in a different direction from the song that singer Dinah Shore had turned into a hit in 1944, "I'll Walk Alone" (by Jule Styne and Sammy Cahn), which dealt with eternal fidelity to an absent loved one.[7] Wartime circumstances had now changed significantly, however. At the time of *Oklahoma!* the likely outcome of World War II was still unclear, but following the D-Day landings on June 6, 1944, the liberation of Paris on August 25, and the Allied progress through Italy, matters were more secure on the European front, while things were also looking better in the Pacific given the US victory in the second Battle of Guam (July 21 to August 10, 1944). Even though the defeat of the Nazis would be celebrated only on May 8, 1945 (some three weeks after the opening of *Carousel*), and VJ Day on September 2, minds at home in the United States had long been turning to a postwar future that seemed both exciting and troubling.

One sign of the shift is provided by those feel-good shows and films from the period dealing with scallywag sailors on leave looking to find someone to love to whom they could soon return in civilian life: Leonard Bernstein's *On the Town* (opened December 28, 1944) and the MGM film musical *Anchors Aweigh* (starring Frank Sinatra, Kathryn Grayson, and Gene Kelly), released in July 1945, are obvious examples. Other musicals of the time dealt with different postwar issues: for example, Irving Berlin's *Annie Get Your Gun*, produced by Rodgers and Hammerstein in 1946 (it opened on May 16), engages both with newly configured gender roles and with the fact that two separate Wild West shows that formerly were bitter rivals must now merge to secure their future. In this context, the much darker *Carousel* starts looking like the other side of the coin. It is easy enough to view

"You'll Never Walk Alone" as reassurance to the war widows left alone to support themselves and their children on inadequate government pensions. However, Billy's redemption, and also Julie's, engages with another social problem that was widely acknowledged at the time.

It is a trope of opera and musical theater that its leading women often fall for the wrong man. In the case of *Show Boat*, Magnolia would have been better off not marrying the rascally Gaylord Ravenal, while in *Oklahoma!* Laurey feels some fascination for Jud, though she quickly sets him aside in disgust. One song in *Show Boat* also dealt with how "lovin' dat man of mine," regardless of whether he is lazy or slow, was unavoidable, just as "fish got to swim" and "birds got to fly." Billy is a far worse case, however, and one wonders what Julie sees in him. Rodgers and Hammerstein appear to have been at a loss: they dropped the idea (in the scenario) of her explaining what her "idea of a man" might be (in the proposed quartet in act 1, scene 3), perhaps because they had no idea what she might say. Her eventual advice on the matter to Carrie also seems problematic. This comes in act 2, scene 1 (on the island), and is consequent upon the changes to that scene once Dwight disappeared from the reckoning.

Carrie and Enoch Snow have had a tiff, and her companions urge her to break off the engagement, arguing that marriage is no boon for women. As we learn in one of the stanzas of "Stonecutters Cut It on Stone":

The clock jest ticks yer life away,
There's no relief in sight.
It's cookin' and scrubbin' and sewin' all day
And Gawd-knows-whatin' all night!

Julie, however, takes a different view in a new song:

> What's the use of wond'rin'
> If he's good or if he's bad,
> . . .
> He's your feller and you love him—
> That's all there is to that.

She sings this "softly and earnestly" in the same key she had used for "If I Loved You" (D-flat major). However, the "swung" melody does not quite square with the stage direction in Hammerstein's final libretto: "as she goes on, she quite obviously becomes autobiographical in her philosophy. Her singing is quiet, almost recited" (see example 5.1 ▶).

Hammerstein later acknowledged his big mistake in this song: ending it with the word "talk," given the problem of

EXAMPLE 5.1 *Carousel*, "What's the Use of Wond'rin'?" (Julie Jordan), mm. 39–44

how to sing the final phoneme (ta-*lk*). This was one reason, he suspected, why "What's the Use of Wond'rin'?" did not do well in terms of sheet-music sales, on record, or on the radio, even though it did "dramatic service" in the play.[8] But there may be other grounds for that. While the "philosophy" in the song does indeed have a bearing on Julie's autobiography—and it moves far beyond any advice Carrie needs to resolve her tiff—it is hardly politically correct by any modern standards:

> Common sense may tell you
> That the endin' will be sad
> And now's the time to break and run away.
> But what's the use of wond'rin'
> If the endin' will be sad?
> He's your feller and you love him—
> There's nothin' more to say.

Julie is a victim of domestic violence, and the ending will indeed "be sad," but is there really "nothin' more to say"?

In the *B* section, Julie acknowledges that "somethin' made him the way that he is." In 1945, that "something" would have been widely acknowledged to be a war that left battle-hardened soldiers, sailors, and airmen struggling to re-enter a civilian life that had changed significantly during their time at the front. The pressures were not just economic but also social and psychological. Thus on Monday May 22, 1944, the *New York Times* carried a report of a sermon just delivered by the Rev. Dr. John Sutherland Bonnell at the Fifth Avenue Presbyterian Church in New York. The demobilization of some ten million servicemen at the close of the war would present "a tremendous challenge to the Christian church":

> The emphasis on educational and vocational rehabilitation must not be allowed to overshadow the profound need that will exist for spiritual reorientation. Inevitably there will exist, to a considerable degree, psychological mal-adjustments manifested in disillusionment, resentment toward civilians, depression, and a sense of guilt. . . . The true glory of peace must be substituted for the transient glamour of war. The aggressive instincts developed in service men must be channeled into a noble crusade against intolerance, ignorance, poverty and hate.

This "educational and vocational rehabilitation" refers to the long discussions in the US government that led to the War Mobilization and Reconversion Act, signed into law on October 3, 1944. While President Roosevelt approved it, he noted for the record, "I feel it my duty to draw attention to the fact that the bill does not adequately deal with the human side of reconversion." The issue also contributed to the massive increase in the number of divorces in 1945–47. Billy Bigelow has all the debilities noted in Bonnell's sermon: maladjustment, disillusionment, resentment, a sense of guilt, and aggressive instincts. Dealing with his "human side" posed profound questions that needed to be answered.[9]

When *Carousel* was staged at London's Royal National Theatre in 1992–93, the acerbic critic Robert Brustein, writing in the *New Republic*, thought that the cloying final scene created "a Rotarian atmosphere congenial to audiences who seek not reality but escape from reality, not truth but respite from truth." One can also see how the show might have become a refuge for scoundrels: not for nothing was *Carousel* the favorite musical of US president Richard Nixon. However, Brustein should have been more sensitive to the "reality" of 1945, when audiences found consolation and even some manner of truth in Rodgers and Hammerstein's conclusion. It might have been acceptable for Jud Fry to stay "daid" at the end of *Oklahoma!* But for better or for worse, his successor, Billy Bigelow, needed a very different outcome.[10]

# CHAPTER 6

# FROM STAGE TO SCREEN (AND BACK)

AN END-OF-WAR CONTEXT FOR *Carousel* explains more than just its handling of the dilemmas posed by its characters; the show also played a significant role in a much broader debate about the potential of American musical theater to move beyond mere entertainment into the realm of art. This too was part of the war effort, not just as Broadway luminaries argued over how best to keep morale high, but also given the role played by culture on the battlefield itself, and in terms of allowing the United States to assert its dominance as a force for good in a postwar world.

Critics reviewing the Boston tryout of *Carousel* had set the tone, as we have seen: the show was "different from conventional musical comedy," certainly a "musical play" or perhaps a "music drama," and maybe even "the beginning of our own authentic American opera." In contrast to the European fare offered in US opera houses—from Mozart through Puccini, with large chunks of Wagner (even during World War II)—Broadway offered the potential for a near-operatic experience that was uniquely "American" in its creation, content, and spirit. Olin Downes had made the argument in connection with *Porgy and Bess* and *Oklahoma!* Kurt Weill also picked up on it in his own statements on the "new" forms of musical theater that he might bring to the New York stage.[1] But those Boston critics were also responding to the remarkably efficient publicity machines operated by the press agents of the Theatre Guild, of Rodgers and Hammerstein, of Rouben Mamoulian, and of anyone else who wanted to take credit for *Carousel.*

## THE SEARCH FOR "AMERICAN OPERA"

Hammerstein had long been interested in what a more "operatic" approach to Broadway musical theater might entail. He wrote in 1925, "The history of musical comedy has passed through a variety of phases, but the type that persists, that shows the signs of ultimate victory, is the operetta—the musical play with music and plot welded together in skillful cohesion." He also asked, "Is there a form of musical play tucked away somewhere . . . which could attain the heights of grand opera and still keep sufficiently human to be entertaining?" His thinking had a significant influence on *Show Boat* (1927), which many came to regard as an important step in this new direction. But what an appropriate "form of musical play" might be remained a matter of debate through the 1930s, as did what would define the result as "American" in terms of setting, theme, plot, and the use of "folk" materials musical or otherwise. The question of race also posed its own challenges and helps explain why Olin Downes and others remained ambivalent about *Porgy and Bess*, despite its favorable reception elsewhere.[2]

Rodgers and Hammerstein's *Oklahoma!* seemed a safer bet, however. According to Downes's essay on the show, published on June 6, 1943, "It is in the field of musical comedy and operetta that we have so far done best and in which . . . we can expect to advance." Even in Europe, he added, it was popular works akin to *Oklahoma!* that had created both "national" and "living" opera. His examples ranged from *The Beggar's Opera* through Mozart's *Die Zauberflöte* and Beethoven's *Fidelio* to Weber's "immortal" *Der Freischütz* and Bizet's *Carmen*. All of those European works combined spoken dialogue with musical numbers, rather than being set to music throughout. The reference to *Fidelio* is also significant: clearly it was a work by a demonstrably "great" composer—perhaps even the greatest—though not one who had achieved success on the operatic stage. It prompted John Gassner to suggest to the Theatre Guild on June 7 (the day after Downes's article appeared) that Virgil Thomson be approached to produce a new adaptation of Beethoven's opera (as "a really unconventional production"), rewriting its libretto and adding some comedy to it.[3]

*Fidelio* also reappears in the run-up to *Carousel*. By now Downes had sufficient confidence in Rodgers and Hammerstein to take the wholly unusual step of puffing the show even before it went on the stage. On December 24, 1944, the *New York Times* published his piece on their "new opera" due, he wrote, in March.[4] According to Rodgers, it would be something very different from *Oklahoma!*

> He and Mr. Hammerstein have undertaken something which can either fail to realize in terms of text and music the poignancy and heartbreak, and the unique blend of realism and fantasy that give Molnar's play such a grip upon the emotions and the memory of anyone who comes under its spell, or something that could surpass in significance anything that our native musical theatre has thus far produced.

Downes does not seem entirely convinced, but he is willing to go along with the argument. He does have one concern, however: "It is no simple proposal to effect an American transposition of the flavor of the play which is so characteristic an expression of central European life and culture without losing the quality of the original." This is the challenge facing Hammerstein.

> Then comes the question of the music, also challenging to a composer of exceptional gifts, but who must go much deeper and farther in the emotional sense than anything he has thus far attempted if he is to intensify by means of his art the drama of Molnar. All this means a new approach to American problems of the lyric stage, and one which can be successful only if conducted in a wholly original and creative spirit.

As for the adaptation:

> The scene of the play is transferred from Hungary to New England of 1870. The characters, says Mr. Rodgers, are not going to be glamour boys and girls—any more than Molnar's were—but the kind of people one would see in an American village or town,

> people old and young, fat and thin, ordinary and queer—the plain stuff of humanity. These will be "folks," American "folks," and, if the composer succeeds, will so express themselves in his music.

Downes's essay continues to extol the evident seriousness of Rodgers's approach. His *Liliom* will have "an orchestra of more nearly symphonic caliber than anything Mr. Rodgers has experimented with before." Rodgers has also decided to dispense with the traditional overture, because no one pays attention to it anyway, although there will be "a big overture summarizing the main musical and dramatic ideas of the drama, before the second part begins." Downes thinks this is a good idea, not only because Puccini, Strauss, and Verdi tended to dispense with overtures but also given that Strauss (in *Elektra* and *Salome*) and Puccini (in *Tosca*) included stretches of "symphonic commentary" later in their operas. But the prime example is, again, *Fidelio*, where the "greatest of all overtures"—the third *Leonore* one—was dropped as a prelude and replaced by the "short Italianate piece" that begins the opera (the *Fidelio* overture), though Downes thinks that it has now found its proper place by commonly being added just before the opera's final scene. However, *Liliom* will have a musical prelude too, representing the waltz music of the carousel, which "will be in itself a complete composition, with balanced parts and form" and will also receive musical intensification in later scenes as the drama demands.

*Fidelio* had not been done at the Metropolitan Opera since March 3, 1941 (and would not be again until March 17, 1945), but Arturo Toscanini conducted two radio broadcasts of Beethoven's opera in December 1944: act 1 on Sunday, December 10, and act 2 a week later, on the 17th. Toscanini did indeed include the *Leonore* Overture no. 3 before the act 2 finale. Clearly the opera was on Downes's mind when he was writing his piece published on the 24th. However, the notion that the "Carousel Waltz" would have a clear, well-rounded form plays into a broader argument about the entire show made by Downes, or by Rodgers speaking through him:

> But the score will be a musical organism. The forms will be essentially melodic and vocal, and not rest for developments upon the orchestra, although that part of the work will be also of much significance. Traditional recitative there will not be, but there will be melodies that develop as the musical fulfillment of speech into tonal structures, in themselves organic, while flexibly responsive to the needs of the situations. In a word, the "statue" will be where it belongs in lyric drama—on the stage, and the pedestal have its place in the orchestra.

Downes may not have believed all this (he ends: "This much Mr. Rodgers told about his forthcoming creation, in which he is intensely and happily engaged"). But the fact that he was willing to relay it is significant enough. His editorializing is also revealing, not least the rather extravagant comparison with Beethoven and his emphasis on *Carousel*'s symphonic conception and organicism on the one hand, and, on the other, the fact that Rodgers had his priorities straight. His lyric drama is right where it belongs: on the stage rather than in the pit. In other words, Rodgers is no Wagner, for which one might reasonably be thankful.

Downes's article is fascinating both for what it says and for what it does not. For example, whatever Rodgers may have planned for the repositioned "overture" to *Carousel*, he never delivered it—the entr'acte music is of the conventional potpourri kind—and no one thought to point out that Kurt Weill's *Lady in the Dark* (1941) had already done something similar with its act 2 "overture" (act 1 begins as if it were a spoken play). More surprising, however, is the fact that while Downes firmly associates Rodgers with the European operatic canon (Verdi, Puccini, Richard Strauss), he does not engage the "American opera" argument he had developed for *Oklahoma!* The fact that *Carousel* was based on a European play—albeit revised to represent "American folks"—may have counted against it in that regard: it is one reason why the show failed to receive the New York Drama Critics' Circle Award for Best American Play of the season, despite some significant pressure, though it did gain a citation for making "an advance in the musical field."[5]

In his conversation with Downes that led to this article, Rodgers does indeed seem to have given him the impression, or did nothing to prevent it, that *Liliom* would be "a new opera" (to quote Downes's headline). But the composer was very savvy when dealing with the press and tended to tailor his remarks to the needs of the moment. For example, less than a month after his interview with Downes, he was telling a somewhat different story to Gertrude Samuels. Here Rodgers presents himself as the model of a hard-working businessman, one contributing to the war effort (he has a victory garden at his country house in Fairfield, Connecticut). His take on musical theater is different too:

> American musical comedy or operetta or folk opera or whatever you want to call musical theatre can be art—and I don't

mean "arty." I don't mean it should imitate the posturings of European grand opera. I mean the writing of music, the designing of clothes and scenery as though they belonged to the characters and the period.

In other texts around this time, Rodgers also sought to come up with a better definition of the "musical play" as it was developing on the American stage. This could not afford to be "simply a warmed-up dish of European traditions" but needed to stem from, and celebrate, indigenous values. Thus Rodgers was ambivalent about Hammerstein's *Carmen Jones* (still playing on Broadway in the run-up to *Carousel*, though it closed on February 10, 1945): it was near perfect in making long-haired opera accessible to a broader audience, but it was "not native."[6] And while Rodgers was happy to pursue the idea of *Carousel* as a new, more sophisticated form of musical play, his rhetoric against it being in any way operatic tended to harden, perhaps because it was untenable, but also, it seems, because the matter was of increasingly less concern as the war drew to a close.

Burton Rascoe, reviewing the Broadway production (*World-Telegram*, April 28, 1945), considered *Carousel* to be an advance over *Show Boat* in terms of "indigenous American opera." However, John Chapman (*Daily News*, April 20) felt that the show "did not fit into the pattern of musical comedy, operetta, opera bouffe or even opera." John Mason Brown (*Saturday Review of Literature*, May 5) followed suit: none of the standard labels for musical theater fit *Carousel*, which could only be described as "a play with music; a play which turns from dialogue to song, and from straight acting into dance, almost without one's being aware of it." Rodgers probably came to regard that last analysis as the best one. In August 1945, Mark A. Schubart asked him about the apparent operatic tendencies in the show, noted somewhat ambivalently by its devotees, and he received a somewhat curt response: Rodgers "isn't interested in opera—folk or otherwise" or in bringing "art" to Broadway, though he did want to give musical theater a seriousness of purpose. For Rodgers, the extensive musical passages in *Carousel* "are simply part of his conception of what a musical Americanized version of Molnar's *Liliom* requires." Schubart did not quite believe him: *Carousel* clearly has elements drawing on opera, he wrote, which is a genre that still has something to offer even if its "present rather stagnant condition" makes it "a retarded and perhaps moribund art." Schubart also went on to note the musical sophistication of the show, proof of which was the fact that the "so-called serious musical world" was starting to pay attention to it, with symphony orchestras programming parts of *Carousel* in their concerts: indeed, "Dr. Serge Koussevitzky himself pronounced the *Carousel* waltzes charming."[7]

Such numbers in *Carousel* as "If I Loved You" and Billy's "Soliloquy" clearly have what many would identify as operatic elements. But even during the Boston tryout, Rodgers worried that associating the show with opera might "scare people off." By August 1945, he was perhaps becoming jaded with the grander claims being made for *Carousel*. Or maybe ticket sales just needed a boost. But the timing is significant in other ways as well, given that World War II was at an end. The focus was now on a postwar future where American art needed neither Old World models nor validation. Schubart said that opera was "stagnant," "retarded," and "moribund," while Stark Young, reviewing *Carousel* in the *New Republic*, did not see much merit in viewing it as approaching opera, or the dancing approaching ballet, given "how third-rate most of the opera and most of the ballet we see is." *Carousel* could now stand on its own.[8]

## CAROUSEL *ON FILM*

*Carousel* ran for 890 performances at the Majestic Theatre, closing on May 24, 1947, a year before *Oklahoma!* (after 2,212 performances). The show embarked on a two-year national tour that began in Chicago on May 29, 1947, then went to fifty-four cities; it returned briefly to the Majestic from February 22 to March 5, 1949, a month before the opening of *South Pacific* there on April 7. The London production opened at the Theatre Royal, Drury Lane, on June 7, 1950 (566 performances); Eric Mattson and Bambi Linn reprised their original roles. Rodgers and Hammerstein also revived *Carousel* at the New York City Center from June 2 to August 8, 1954, as they had done with *Oklahoma!* the previous year. By then they had purchased the Theatre Guild's rights to all three shows done with them (the third was *Allegro*).

Despite frequent early approaches from Hollywood studios, Rodgers and Hammerstein were reluctant to sanction film versions of shows that were still making money on Broadway or on tour. Nor did they want to share with the Guild any profits that might come from the silver screen, which is in part why they bought the rights. But the idea of turning to film had been in play at least since 1950, and Metro-Goldwyn-Mayer's palpable successes (thanks to

Arthur Freed) with such transfers as Irving Berlin's *Annie Get Your Gun* (1946) in 1950, Cole Porter's *Kiss Me, Kate* (1948) in 1953, and Lerner and Loewe's *Brigadoon* (1947) in 1954 had put Rodgers and Hammerstein under some pressure. They may also have feared that they were losing their Broadway touch when neither *Me and Juliet* (1953) nor *Pipe Dream* (1955) swept the boards. Work had already begun in secret on a screenplay for *Oklahoma!* in early 1953; shooting took place over the second half of 1954 (Fred Zinnemann was the director); and the film was released on October 11, 1955. By then, *Carousel* (directed by Henry King) was well into production; it had parallel premieres in New York and Los Angeles on February 16, 1956.

The film version of *Oklahoma!* was co-produced by the Magna Theatre Corporation and Rodgers & Hammerstein Productions. *Carousel* was done by Twentieth Century–Fox, however, which announced its purchase of the rights on June 30, 1955.[9] The switch was caused by contractual issues involving Molnár's play (which Fox Studios had filmed in 1930); it also meant that *Carousel* had a smaller budget than *Oklahoma!* ($3.38 million versus $6.8 million). Billy Bigelow was to be played by Frank Sinatra (see figure 6.1), typecast as yet another character of dubious morals: he was Nathan Detroit in the 1955 film of *Guys and Dolls* and played the lead in the 1957 *Pal Joey*. Sinatra pre-recorded Billy's songs for the soundtrack, but he quit early on when he learned that he would have to do everything twice for filming in two wide-screen formats: CinemaScope (35 mm) and CinemaScope 55 (*Oklahoma!* also came out in two such formats: Todd-AO and CinemaScope). However, Shirley Jones (who played Julie) said that Ava Gardner, Sinatra's

FIGURE 6.1 Costume photograph for Frank Sinatra as Billy Bigelow intended for the film version of *Carousel*. Courtesy of Rodgers & Hammerstein: An Imagem Company, www.rnh.com

wife at the time, had also pressured him to leave.[10] A million-dollar lawsuit with the studio ensued. By late August 1955, when shooting had already begun, Gordon MacRae had replaced Sinatra to star alongside Jones, as they had already done in the film of *Oklahoma!* (as Curly and Laurey). Location filming took place in Boothbay Harbor and elsewhere in Maine, and in Paradise Cove in California for Billy's "Soliloquy" and parts of "Louise's Ballet."

*Oklahoma!* transferred fairly easily to the silver screen, with just two songs omitted (one was Jud's "Lonely Room," a significant loss). The screenwriters for *Carousel*, Phoebe and Henry Ephron, had a harder time of it, however. Hollywood and Broadway had long had a complex relationship when it came to musical theater, both economically (as the studios lured stars from the stage) and aesthetically. The rise on Broadway of the "integrated" musical was due at least in part to Hollywood having developed a monopoly on other, more conventional music-theatrical genres (such as the revue or the backstage musical) that could be done to far more spectacular effect on a studio set. However, the medium of film retained certain canons of verisimilitude—matters needed to be "lifelike"—and also depended on audiences imagining themselves in the middle of the action in ways that made singing problematic unless it could somehow be done in realistic circumstances. *Annie Get Your Gun* transferred well enough to film in 1950 as it was a "backstage musical" of sorts (hence "There's No Business Like Show Business"), as did *Show Boat* (in 1951) and *Kiss Me, Kate* (1953) for similar reasons. Lerner and Loewe's *Brigadoon* (1954), on the other hand, relied on its fantastical plot and exotic location to allow Gene Kelly to sing to, and then dance with, Cyd Charisse in "The Heather on the Hill."

The darker *Carousel* had no such advantages. The Ephrons therefore adopted a different strategy, creating a pre-credit sequence in which we see Billy polishing stars "up there," as we assume he has been doing for fifteen years. The Heavenly Friend interrupts his work—for "things ain't going so good for your kinfolk down on earth"—telling him of the chance to go back for a day. The new invention continues after the credits: Billy goes to see the Starkeeper, who reminds him that he had already turned down the one-day offer on his arrival. However, an exception can be made if there is some justification for it, and he invites Billy to tell his life story. The "Carousel Waltz" then leads us "down here" to the start of the play, but now also back in time. As a result, the action up to Billy's death is shown as a flashback, while his later scene with the Starkeeper brings us back to the present, as does Billy's final day on earth.

One reason for that flashback structure, it was said, was to prevent audiences thinking that the film ended with Billy's death. However, it also makes the presence of music more plausible: it may still not be "real," but it becomes part and parcel of Billy's embellishing the whole story to his advantage. In effect, the film of *Carousel* reverses the strategy of *The Wizard of Oz*, with a fantasy musical world located under, rather than over, the rainbow. Other changes to the stage version can probably be ascribed to different cinematic sensibilities: for example, Billy's death is played as an accident rather than a suicide, and the Starkeeper also ties up a loose end left in the libretto (though not in Hammerstein's scenario) involving what happens to Jigger Craigin. Likewise, the screenplay solved one problem of the ending, whether Billy's gestures to Louise and Julie are sufficient to gain redemption, by placing less emphasis on any formal requirement for him to do something "good" for them in the first place: he already has a job polishing stars to which he presumably can return.

Still other changes come back to the role of the music, however. The first part of the "Julie and Carrie Sequence" (with "You're a queer one, Julie Jordan") and "Blow High, Blow Low" ended on the cutting-room floor for reasons of time, although they both appear on the soundtrack recording. So too does a stanza cut from "Stonecutters Cut It on Stone" (the one given in chapter 5), probably for fear of the censors given its reference to women having to do "Gawd-knows-whatin' all night!" Other songs had already been removed from the screenplay, including the reprise of "Mister Snow," "Geraniums in the Winder," and "The Highest Judge of All." "When the Children Are Asleep" was shifted to a boat ride to the island and sung in the presence of Billy and Julie. Other revisions removed still more music such as linking passages and the like, turning the show into more of a sequence of discrete numbers. The fact that Agnes de Mille was not involved in the choreography (done instead by Rod Alexander, Bambi Linn's husband at the time) also bothered her deeply in the years to come, even though she did receive screen credit for the original design of "Louise's Ballet."[11] She was not alone in thinking that the end result was something of a travesty in terms both of the detail and as a whole: it is not surprising that the main 1956 Academy Award nominations went to the film of *The King and I*, made hard on the heels of *Carousel* and released just four months later, on June 29, 1956.

## *RESTORING* CAROUSEL

Frank Sinatra did end up singing "If I Loved You" with Shirley Jones, on television in a Valentine's Day episode of the *Frank Sinatra Show* (February 14, 1958). He also made at least three recordings of "Soliloquy," one before and two after his aborted appearance in the film. "You'll Never Walk Alone" was picked up by Sinatra as well as by a number of other major performers, including Doris Day, Judy Garland, Elvis Presley, and Andy Williams. It also became an inspirational anthem for numerous sports teams and similar organizations: the fans of Liverpool Football Club (inspired by the 1963 recording by Gerry and the Pacemakers) are just one of many such groups across the world that sing it before home games. The song gained still more resonance after the 1989 disaster when Liverpool supporters died in a crush at Hillsborough Stadium in Sheffield at a match between Liverpool and Nottingham Forest, as it also did when Barbra Streisand sang it at the 2001 Emmy Awards in honor of the victims of the September 11 attacks on the United States. Renée Fleming chose it as well for the Concert for America on the first anniversary of 9/11, but she then turned the song to more aspirational ends at the inauguration ceremony for President Barack Obama in early 2009.

By then, *Carousel* had reestablished its presence on the stage. The 1954 revival was followed by a short run in September 1957 under the auspices of the New York City Center Light Opera Company (which had also done the 1954 production), with Howard Keel as Billy Bigelow and Barbara Cook as Julie Jordan. Jan Clayton reprised her role as Julie in a production at the World's Fair in Brussels in June 1958, and John Raitt returned as Billy at New York's Lincoln Center in August 1965. The show also remained (and remains) popular in regional productions, as well as among amateur societies and college and high-school groups. However, Nicholas Hytner probably thought of it as a neglected masterpiece when he directed a production of *Carousel* at London's Royal National Theatre in late 1992. The RNT had already extended its reach beyond straight plays with a sensational production of *Guys and Dolls* in 1982, and its *Carousel* was part of a season set to include Stephen Sondheim's *Sweeney Todd*. Clearly there was some box-office opportunism here—and a few RNT patrons sniffed at the apparent decline in standards—but the argument that select Broadway musicals merited mounting on what was otherwise considered a stage for high-art drama had a significant impact on the genre. It also enabled some theatrical reimagining of the show itself: for example, Hytner began the prologue with Julie stuck in mindless drudgery at her loom in the mill until being liberated by the end-of-work bell.[12]

The RNT *Carousel* had a classy cast—including the black actor Clive Rowe as Enoch Snow—and new choreography by Kenneth MacMillan, the principal choreographer of the Royal Ballet (who died very shortly before the production opened). It ran to sellout audiences from December 1992 to March 1993 and then transferred to the Shaftesbury Theatre in London's West End from September 1993 to May 1994, reaping a slew of Olivier Awards. The transatlantic transfer to the Vivian Beaumont Theatre at Lincoln Center—with a white Enoch Snow but a black Carrie Pipperidge, the award-winning Audra McDonald—was also regarded as a success. Its 337 performances from March 24, 1994, to January 15, 1995, ran somewhat shorter than the RNT's later *Oklahoma!* (1998; directed by Trevor Nunn) at the Gershwin Theatre in 2002–3, with 388 performances and then a highly successful tour. Both were far exceeded by the new production of *South Pacific* at Lincoln Center in 2008–10 (996 performances). These numbers suggest that

*Time* magazine's designation of *Carousel* in 1999 as the "best musical of the twentieth century" reflected esteem more than popularity.

But esteem counts for something. It also helps explain why *Carousel*, unlike *Oklahoma!* and *South Pacific*, has followed *Show Boat* onto operatic stages in the United States, with recent productions by, for example, Virginia Opera (May 2013), Jacksonville Opera Theatre (Alabama; May 2014), the Glimmerglass Festival (summer 2014), a co-production between the Chicago Lyric Opera (April–May 2015) and Houston Grand Opera (April–May 2016), and the Utah Festival Opera (summer 2015). Something similar has occurred in the United Kingdom as well (Opera North in 2012 and the English National Opera in 2017). This is by no means a new phenomenon: Houston Grand Opera did *Carousel* in June 1990 (following a number of other Broadway classics). For that matter, in 1955 RCA Victor released a studio recording of *Carousel* with renowned opera singers Robert Merrill and Patrice Munsel as Billy and Julie. Clearly opera companies, like highbrow theatrical ones, now need money-spinners. But they also continue the quest for that ever elusive genre: America opera. Not for nothing has *Carousel* gained keynote status, not just within the world of Broadway musical theater but beyond.

**APPENDIX**

# HAMMERSTEIN'S SCENARIO FOR *CAROUSEL*

THIS FOUR-PAGE TYPESCRIPT SURVIVES in LC/OH; the collection is currently unprocessed and therefore does not yet have any systematic numbering of its contents.

In this transcription, Hammerstein's spellings have been retained, although the layout and punctuation have been rationalized, as have the stylings (for example, in the document song titles are given in upper case and underlined), and typographical errors are silently corrected. The text has some occasional deletions (with text overtyped by Xs); they are not transcribed here. All editorial insertions are indicated by square brackets. Notes cued here (a, b, c . . . ) come at the end of the appendix.

## *LILIOM OUTLINE*

(Song Titles Tentative, merely indicate idea for memorandum. Ditto names of scenes & characters.)

ACT ONE

SCENE 1: Merry-Go-Round.

"Waltz Suite"—Ensemble Pantomime, introducing characters.

SCENE 2: Park—or A Path Near The Shore.

Muskat threatens Julie. Marie on too. Liliom enters, opposes Muskat and she fires him. She exits. Later Liliom exits. Marie now confides her problem, now that she knows that Julie has one. Should Marie choose Solid & Sensible Wolf, or Romantic and Unreliable Dwight?

"What's on Your Mind?" —Duet: Marie & Julie, and "occasionals."

(When you work at the loom or spindle? When you lie awake at night? When you rise at six? etc.) Marie confesses frankly. Julie reveals her feelings by implications. Occasional girls insert line for laugh or punctuation.

Liliom comes back, Marie exits. Liliom & Julie start scene, interrupted by Mill Owner crossing and firing Julie. Now they are both fired. Their scene drifts from dialogue into singing, eventually developing into a major refrain.

"The Wind Blows the Blossoms"—Duet: Liliom & Julie.

(And they fly before they fall.)

SCENE 3: Pier Restaurant.

"Bustin' Out All Over!"—Mill Owner & Ensemble.

(The sap is runnin', the buds are poppin', I'm full o' ginger and my gal's full o' beans, cows're jumpin' fences and the bees're busier'n I ever see 'em before . . . )

"Sand Dance"[a]

Julie, Hollunder, maybe Marie & Dwight. Dwight exits. Two girls discuss Julie's problem with her husband, Liliom, and Marie's problem. If Dwight passes through, take him off so that only girls are on to lead into Holl[under]'s number:

"Just As If It Happened to Me"—Hollunder. (When a sparrow falls I'm hurt, when a child laughs I'm happy.) The character who lives her whole life vicariously.

Liliom & Ficsur. Liliom rejects hold-up scheme, here described by Ficsur in some detail, hooking it up with clam-bake & treasure hunt.

"Sea Chanty"—Ficsur, Liliom & Men.

Wolf & Marie.

"Put Your Faith in Sardines and Me"[b]—Wolf & Marie.

Marie, Julie, Muskat, Hollunder.

"That's My Idea of a Man"—Quartette. Form of *Desert Song* Number. Each soloist getting a chance, probably augment with girls cho[rus].[c]

Muskat & Liliom. She tries to lure him back. Julie insists on talking to him alone. Muskat exits. Julie tells him she's going to have a baby. Leaves him alone.

"I'm Going to Have a Baby!"—Liliom.

After Number crowd comes on, ready to get into boats and go out to islands. Mill Owner with them.[d] Loud and lusty reprise:

"Finale: Bustin' Out All Over"—Entire Company.

Julie happy, not realizing what Liliom is saying to Ficsur in corner. Obviously he has changed his mind. He will go ahead with Ficsur's scheme. He must get money for his wife and baby and take them to New York! If this can not be made clear in pantomime—and it probably can't—there is no reason why Ficsur can't come on before crowd for a scene with Liliom before the finale gets under way.

ACT TWO

SCENE 1: Island.

"A Song Drifts Over the Bay"—Ensemble & Principals.
(Quiet, beautifully harmonized "Just a song at twilight" type.[e])

All exit, to get clues for treasure hunt. Marie is detained by Dwight and his guitar. Wolf enters and demands a show down. Lead into "Marchbanks Song."

"Here's What I Can Give You"—Marie, Wolf & Dwight.

(Each makes his bid, as in *Candida*.[f]) Finally Marie, thrilled by Dwight's music, succumbs to Wolf! (*Cyrano*)[g]

They exit on number. Liliom & Ficsur come on. Rehearsal. Problem of knife. They take bread knife used by Julie for sandwiches. Julie on. Tries to dissuade Liliom for [= from] going without her on hunt. Distrusts Ficsur, scents something wrong. Liliom resists. Crowd on, celebrating Marie's announcement she is to marry Wolf. All ready to start on hunt. Julie joins gay wishes to Marie, but in midst of all, after Liliom & Ficsur gone, discovers bread knife missing!

"Finaletto"

(Containing substance described above.)

SCENE 2: Culvert.

Action as is. Possibly "mystic" number based on reflections in early part of scene. Card Game to be scored with dialogue and each gesture synchronized to music.

SCENE 3: Pier Restaurant. Possibly, even probably Interior.

"Reprise: Bustin' Out All Over"

Crowd back. When noise at height, Liliom brought in by police!

Scene. Consolation. Everyone wants to be "right," as Liliom used to say. All off but Julie who stands over his body. Hollunder in b.g. [background] comes forward slowly.

"Female Duet"—Holl[under] & Julie.

a. Holl[under]—"lullaby" quality. Holds Julie on her lap.
b. Content of Molnar's speech & memory of little inconsequential and "funny" things about Liliom.

Meanwhile the Heavenly Policemen come in and take him. He stops on the way out, listens to Julie & smiles. He is off before curtain. Both women singin[g] at curtain.

SCENE 4: In Transit.

Liliom & Two Policemen on three merry-go-round horse[s], pointing upward. Horses have wings. He sees the next 17 years. Reprises and new music, singing, dialogue, pantomime & dancing are all used throughout this sequence. The baby is born, Ficsur is hanged. The baby grows to a child. Wolf & Marie get richer and increase their family steadily. Dwight keeps strumming along[.] Julie keeps turning carpenter down. The child is a young woman. Bambi![h] Dance! Liliom wants to go back! Can't. Organ! Pearly Gate.

SCENE 5: Front Parlor.

The organ diminishes to a more reedy quality. Lights come up on a woman playing a harmonium. She is an old and very wise looking woman. Liliom is ushered in and they have a nice talk and then her husband comes in. It develops that God is a married couple. They talk over all problems together. A woman's viewpoint is needed as well as a man's. They decide that Liliom should be allowed to go back and see his daughter and prove that he has changed—tho he is no more repentant than in the Molnar version. A simple little song may be sung to harmonium accompaniment in this scene.

"Life Is As Simple As You Make It"—Mr. & Mrs. G. & Liliom.

Whether or not we shall have other characters in this scene will be determined later. Liliom steals a cookie shaped like a star before he goes—or is it a star that looks like a cookie?

SCENE 6: Louise's bedroom.

Julie is helping her dress for her graduation exercises. Liliom comes on with the cookie-star. Same content as now—whatever musical reprises that may be appropriate.

"Reprises"—Julie? Liliom? Louise?

SCENE 7: Outside Schoolhouse—On the Lawn.

The local minister is finishing his address. Julie looks on. So do Marie & Wolf, with their progeny. So does Holl[under], vicariously enjoying it.

"Graduation Song: Finale"

The girls, all in white organdy, holding bouquets, start to sing. Liliom looks on. The organ plays, and their voices sound not unlike angels. The heavenly policeman who came down accompanying Liliom nods to him He starts to go with him. The voices swell loud and gay. There is hope for all these young girls, and for Louise too, even though Liliom was her father. Julie looks tearfully happy and probably wishes Liliom could be there to see it. The sun is shining and the singing continues, sweet and celestial as the curtain falls.

Second curtain, the group breaks and all join their respective families and there are shouts and congratulations and laughter and kisses. Liliom leaves for good now. The curtain falls on the gay picture.

a The "Sand Dance" lasted into the draft libretto dated January 9, 1945: the men track sand up from the beach where they have been digging for clams, and the women use brooms and brushes to sweep it off the stage. Hammerstein imagined it as a typical soft-shoe shuffle.

b Compare Enoch Snow's claims in the libretto (act 1, scene 3) that he will package herrings as sardines and get rich on them.

c Sigmund Romberg. *The Desert Song* (1926), with lyrics by Otto Harbach and a book by Harbach, Oscar Hammerstein II, and Frank Mandel. Hammerstein is probably referring to "Romance" for Margot and a female chorus in act 1 (no. 8), where Margot describes what she longs for in a man.

d So Hammerstein is unclear on whom Liliom and Ficsúr will rob in act 2.

e James Lynam Molloy (1837–1909), "Love's Old Sweet Song" ("Just a Song at Twilight"), with lyrics by Clifton Bingham (1859–1913).

f George Bernard Shaw's *Candida* (1903) is about the wife of clergyman James Mavor Morell tempted to run off with the poet Eugene Marchbanks but in the end deciding to stay in her marriage. On Broadway, the lead role was often associated with Katharine Cornell, who starred in it in December 1924–April 1925, then produced and played in revivals in March–May 1937, April–May 1942, and April–May 1946. The name of Candida's would-be lover explains Hammerstein's reference to a "Marchbanks Song." *The Desert Song* has a similar number—Margot's "I Want a Kiss" (no. 10)—as she plays off her suitors Paul and Pierre.

g In Edmond Rostand's play *Cyrano de Bergerac* (1897), the ugly Cyrano uses his eloquence to help the handsome Christian de Neuvillette woo Roxane and eventually gains her love for himself. The actor Walter Hampden made the role his own in performances on Broadway in 1923, 1926, 1928, 1932, and 1936.

h Bambi Linn.

# ADDITIONAL SOURCES FOR READING, LISTENING, AND VIEWING

*Carousel* is often discussed in surveys of the Broadway musical such as Ethan Mordden, *Beautiful Mornin': The Broadway Musical in the 1940s* (New York: Oxford University Press, 1999); Geoffrey Block, *Enchanted Evenings: The Broadway Musical from "Show Boat" to Sondheim and Lloyd Webber*, 2nd ed. (New York: Oxford University Press, 2009); and Larry Stempel, *Showtime: A History of the Broadway Musical Theater* (New York: W. W. Norton, 2010). The most complete archival study of the show to date is David Mark D'Andre, "The Theatre Guild, *Carousel*, and the Cultural Field of American Musical Theatre" (Ph.D. dissertation, Yale University, 2000), while broader aesthetic issues are raised in Scott McMillin, *The Musical as Drama: A Study of the Principles and Conventions behind Musical Shows from Kern to Sondheim* (Princeton, NJ: Princeton University Press, 2006). For Rodgers and Hammerstein, the most useful accounts are Geoffrey Block, *Richard Rodgers* (New Haven, CT: Yale University Press, 2003); Hugh Fordin, *Getting to Know Him: A Biography of Oscar*

*Hammerstein* (New York: Random House, 1977); and Meryle Secrest, *Somewhere for Me: A Biography of Richard Rodgers* (New York: Alfred A. Knopf, 2001). Kara Anne Gardner, *Agnes de Mille: Telling Stories in Broadway Dance* (New York: Oxford University Press, 2016) also has valuable information on *Carousel*.

Various autobiographies by the key players in the creation of the show offer first-hand testimony but need to be treated with the caution customary for any personal memoirs: Agnes de Mille's two autobiographies (1952, 1958), reprinted as *"Dance to the Piper" and "And Promenade Home": A Two-Part Autobiography* (New York: Da Capo, 1979); Theresa Helburn, *A Wayward Quest: The Autobiography of Theresa Helburn* (Boston: Little, Brown, 1960); Lawrence Langner, *The Magic Curtain: The Story of a Life in Two Fields, Theatre and Invention, by the Founder of the Theatre Guild* (New York: Dutton, 1951); Richard Rodgers, *Musical Stages: An Autobiography*, 2nd ed. (Cambridge, MA: Da Capo, 2002). There are useful extracts from some of these and other texts in Geoffrey Block, ed., *The Richard Rodgers Reader* (New York: Oxford University Press, 2002).

Molnár's play is best read in light of the complex historical and social circumstances of Budapest outlined in István Várkonyi, *Ferenc Molnar and the Austro-Hungarian "Fin de Siècle"* (New York: Peter Lang, 1992). Other works with direct bearing on *Carousel* are discussed in Tim Carter, *"Oklahoma!": The Making of an American Musical* (New Haven, CT: Yale University Press, 2007), and Todd R. Decker, *"Show Boat": Performing Race in an American Musical* (New York: Oxford University Press, 2013). The broader wartime context is covered in Annegret Fauser, *Sounds of War: Music in the United States during World War II* (New York: Oxford University Press, 2013). Information on Broadway productions of *Carousel* (and also *Liliom*) can most easily be gleaned from the Internet Broadway Database at www.ibdb.com; however, the Playbill Vault at www.playbillvault.com is starting to rival it as a more reliable source, and it also offers some access to programs for specific performances.

The 1930 film of *Liliom* is available on DVD in the twelve-disc boxed set *Murnau, Borzage, and Fox* (Los Angeles: Twentieth Century–Fox Home Entertainment, 2008); Fritz Lang's 1934 film is commercially available (New York: Kino on Video, 2004); and there are various releases of the 1956 film of *Carousel*, which is also included in *The Rodgers & Hammerstein Collection* (Los Angeles: Twentieth Century–Fox Home Entertainment, 2006). A film of the stage version starring Hugh Jackman (building on his success as Curly in *Oklahoma!*) has reportedly been in pre-production for some time.

CD releases of the original-cast recording (Decca Album DA 400) of the first (1945) production (Universal City, CA: MCA Classics, 1993; MCAD-10799) and of the 1956 film (New York: Angel, 2001; 7243-52735228) can easily be found. The 1945 one omits a fair amount of music (including "Louise's Ballet") but allows a sense of the original voices; the 1956 one includes material cut from the film itself. Some creative internet searching will turn up various links to Jan Clayton and John Raitt's performance of "If I Loved You," and John Raitt's of "Soliloquy," during the *General Foods 25th Anniversary Show: A Salute to Rodgers and Hammerstein* broadcast on all the major television networks on March 28, 1954 (for example, on YouTube: www.youtube.com/watch?v=gfCyUugiWm8 and youtu.be/CKCUapUEFkY) and to various recordings of songs from *Carousel* by Frank Sinatra and others.

# NOTES

## CHAPTER 1

1 Ethan Mordden, *Beautiful Mornin': The Broadway Musical in the 1940s* (New York: Oxford University Press, 1999), 83–89; Larry Stempel, *Showtime: A History of the Broadway Musical Theater* (New York: W. W. Norton, 2010), 335–59; Geoffrey Block, *Enchanted Evenings: The Broadway Musical from "Show Boat" to Sondheim and Lloyd Webber*, 2nd ed. (New York: Oxford University Press, 2009), 195–214; Joseph P. Swain, *The Broadway Musical: A Critical and Musical Survey*, 2nd ed. (Lanham, MD: Scarecrow, 2002), 109–38; Scott McMillin, *The Musical as Drama: A Study of the Principles and Conventions behind Musical Shows from Kern to Sondheim* (Princeton, NJ: Princeton University Press, 2006), 134–39 (and elsewhere). Swain's reading sometimes has the problem of reading too much into musical commonplaces; his reliance on the 1945 vocal score (which did not always accurately reflect what was done onstage) is also bothersome. As for the important studies of musical theater that give relatively little space to *Carousel*, see Raymond Knapp, *The American Musical and the Formation of National Identity* (Princeton, NJ: Princeton University Press, 2005), and *The American Musical and the Formation of Personal Identity* (Princeton, NJ: Princeton University Press, 2006), and Stacy Wolf, *Changed for Good: A Feminist History of the Broadway Musical* (New York: Oxford University Press, 2011).

2 Richard Rodgers, *Musical Stages: An Autobiography*, 2nd ed. (Cambridge, MA: Da Capo, 2002), 243.

## CHAPTER 2

1 Ferenc Molnár, *Liliom: Egy csirkefogó élete és halála—Külvárosi legenda hét képben* (Budapest: Franklin-Társulat, 1909); revised for the German stage by Alfred Polgar as *Liliom: Vorstadt-Legende in 7 Bildern und einem szenischen Prolog* (Vienna: Deutsch-Oesterreichischer Verlag, 1912); translated by Benjamin F. Glazer as *Liliom: A Legend in Seven Scenes and a Prologue* (New York: Boni & Liveright, 1921). Glazer's preface to the 1921 edition summarizes the reception of the play but ignores the German version; for a better overview of the playwright's career, see Louis Rittenberg, "Ferenc Molnár: A Portrait," in Ferenc Molnár, *The Plays of Ferenc Molnár* (New York: Vanguard, 1929), xi–xxii. For Hart's involvement in the translation, see Gary Marmorstein, *A Ship without a Sail: The Life of Lorenz Hart* (New York: Simon & Schuster, 2012), 76–77.

2 Rodgers, *Musical Stages*, 237–38. Broadway productions of *Liliom* can be tracked on www.ibdb.com. The Campbell Playhouse broadcast is available at the Internet Archive, archive.org/details/otr_campbellplayhouse.

3 Bennett A. Cerf and Van H. Cartmell, eds., *Sixteen Famous European Plays* (Garden City, NY: Garden City, 1943), xix–xx.

4 He is called Wolf Berkowitz in the 1921 cast list; the confusion seems to arise from the character named just Berkowics in the Hungarian and German versions of the play, who is a police detective and appears only in scene 1.

5 Mathis's script is in the New York State Archives (Albany), Motion Picture Scripts Collection, no. 016879-2839.

6 Michael Slowik, *After the Silents: Hollywood Film Music in the Early Sound Era, 1926–1934* (New York: Columbia University Press, 2014), 120–25.

7 Patrick McGilligan, *Fritz Lang: The Nature of the Beast* (New York: St. Martin's, 1997), 201.

8 For this exchange (from which I quote, below), see David Mark D'Andre, "The Theatre Guild, *Carousel*, and the Cultural Field of American Musical Theatre" (Ph.D. dissertation, Yale University, 2000), 4–20, drawing on the contents of B/TG, Box 235 (in the new numbering), folder "Kurt Weill." There are other relevant letters in Lys Symonette and Kim H. Kowalke, eds., *Speak Low (When You Speak Love): The Letters of Kurt Weill and Lotte Lenya* (Berkeley: University of California Press, 1996), 208–26.

9 Tim Carter, "Celebrating the Nation: Kurt Weill, Paul Green, and the Federal Theatre Project (1937)," *Journal of the Society for American Music* 5 (2011): 297–334, at 320 (Weill and Meredith considering forming a new production company for "Ballad Theatre"); Symonette and Kowalke, *Speak Low*, 220 (*Liliom* in Berlin). Weill eventually told Helburn (in his letter of March 20, 1937) that Karl Heinz Martin had suggested a musical *Liliom* to him. At some point, Molnár also seems to have rejected an approach from George Gershwin; see Lawrence

Langner's letter to Alan Jay Lerner of June 8, 1956, given in D'Andre, "Theatre Guild," 256–57 (and compare Rodgers, *Musical Stages*, 238).

10 So Weill wrote to Lotte Lenya on May 18, 1945; Symonette and Kowalke, *Speak Low*, 459–60.

11 Tim Carter, *"Oklahoma!": The Making of an American Musical* (New Haven, CT: Yale University Press, 2007), 19 (Hammerstein's flops), 28–31 (Helburn's early thoughts), 34–38 (Hart, with Hammerstein playing along).

12 Carter, *Oklahoma!*, 7 (Molnár), 138–67 (rehearsals and tryouts), 206–7 (Downes), 293 (Toscanini); Nelson B. Bell, "A New Dog Star Appears in Filmdom's Firmament," *Washington Post*, November 8, 1943 (*Noah's Ark*); D'Andre, "Theatre Guild," 168–69 (next-day approval).

## CHAPTER 3

1 B/TG, Box 77, folder "Gassner Memos 1942–3"; "Screen News," *NYT*, June 16, 1943 (*State Fair*); "Theatre Guild May Do *State Fair* As Musical," *Los Angeles Times*, June 30, 1943; Annegret Fauser, "'Dixie *Carmen*': War, Race, and Identity in Oscar Hammerstein's *Carmen Jones* (1943)," *Journal of the Society for American Music* 4 (2010): 127–74. Rodgers and Hammerstein were halfway through their work on *State Fair* in April 1944 (Fred Stanley, "Hollywood Woos South America," *NYT*, April 9, 1944) and had completed it by early May (Leonard Lyons, "Gossip from Gotham," *Washington Post*, May 15, 1944). The film was released in August 1945.

2 "What's New on the Rialto?", *NYT*, June 25, 1944 (no plans; *Liliom* for winter); B/TG, Boxes 172–73, folder "Carousel" (yellow tab; contract); Oscar Hammerstein II, "Turns on a Carousel: An Account of Adventures in Setting the Play *Liliom* to Music," *NYT*, April 15, 1945 (January 1944); D'Andre, "Theatre Guild," 171–75 (production meetings); "Jaffe in *Svoboda* Arriving Tonight," *NYT*, March 1, 1944 (announcement); John Chapman, "Theater Guild Vision Is American Operetta Series," *Chicago Daily Tribune*, July 16, 1944 (fall; Langner says that *Liliom* is "almost completed"). Lawrence Langner later wrote in his autobiography that it took nine months of discussion to get Rodgers and Hammerstein to agree to adapting *Liliom*; see Geoffrey Block, ed., *The Richard Rodgers Reader* (New York: Oxford University Press, 2002), 121. Leonard Lyons, "Broadway Potpourri," *Washington Post*, October 26, 1944, reports that all the "legal technicalities" over *Liliom* have now been resolved after fifteen months.

3 Hammerstein explained his thinking on the locations in "Mr. Hammerstein's Report on *Carousel*," *Boston Post*, March 25, 1945; see also D'Andre, "Theatre Guild," 171 (Hungarian setting), 174 (dialect), 175 (New England).

4 Carter, *Oklahoma!*, 23–24.

5 Olin Downes, "Broadway's Gift to Opera," *NYT*, June 6, 1943 (integrated and indigenous; *Porgy and Bess* not important); Downes, "Roots of Native Opera: Popular Theatre May Prove Forerunner of Genuine American Style," *NYT*, October 27, 1935 (*Porgy and Bess*). For Downes's comments on *Carousel*, see chapter 6.

6 Hammerstein, "Turns on a Carousel" (Maine); D'Andre, "Theatre Guild," 177–80 (research).

7 However, Rodgers and Hammerstein returned to that down-home idiom in *South Pacific*, particularly for Nellie Forbush (from Little Rock, Arkansas) and Joseph Cable. The *State Fair* songs "It Might As Well Be Spring" (which won an Academy Award) and "That's for Me" bear strong similarities, respectively, to Forbush's "A Cockeyed Optimist" and Cable's "My Girl Back Home."

8 Carter, *Oklahoma!*, 149 ($82,000); LC/RM, Box 101, folder 10 (budget for *Carousel*).

9 D'Andre, "Theatre Guild," 174 (reporting on the second production meeting on January 20, 1944).

10 Hugh Fordin, *Getting to Know Him: A Biography of Oscar Hammerstein* (New York: Random House, 1977), 222, notes work on an (unspecified) outline in the summer. D'Andre, "Theatre Guild," 185n22, mentions the present scenario but does not discuss it.

11 Oscar Hammerstein II, "Notes on Lyrics" (1949), in *Lyrics by Oscar Hammerstein II*, ed. William Hammerstein (Milwaukee, WI: Hal Leonard, 1985), 15–16.

12 Molnár has Liliom in the "crimson fire" for sixteen years, and Rodgers and Hammerstein kept switching between seventeen and fifteen, before settling on the latter. They may have been worried about how Louise might appear when played by the dancer Bambi Linn (who turned nineteen in 1945), on the one hand, and, on the other, the likely age of her "graduation," which already involved some creative rethinking of the typical school-leaving age of the period.

13 The scripts are in LC/OH. There are also two copies of the January 1945 one in LC/RM, Box 102, folders 6–7. By now, the names of the characters had changed to their later form, although we have Wilbur Snow and (for Ficsúr) Tom Trainor. Those two were changed late because of potential confusion with the lieutenant governor of Connecticut, Charles Wilbert Snow, and the recently deceased war correspondent, Tom Treanor; see "News and Gossip of the Rialto," *NYT*, March 4, 1945.

14 "The Theatre," *Wall Street Journal*, January 4, 1945 (change of title); "News and Gossip of the Rialto," *NYT*, March 4, 1945 (spelling); "Nine Attractions Set for January," *NYT*, December 30, 1944 (Mamoulian has signed); LC/RM, Box 101,

folder 10 (contract, prepared on December 7), and Box 16, folder 3 (meeting on August 15, 1944; cast audition); "Gossip of the Rialto," *NYT*, June 18, 1944 (hoping for de Mille); Hedda Hopper, "Looking at Hollywood," *Chicago Daily Tribune*, November 21, 1944 (de Mille has agreed). In March–May 1944, the Theatre Guild tried to interest Elia Kazan in directing the show, as he did for Kurt Weill's *One Touch of Venus* in late 1943; D'Andre, "Theatre Guild," 213–15. However, this was probably just a case of hedging bets in case Mamoulian became unavailable.

15 Hedda Hopper, "Looking at Hollywood," *Los Angeles Times*, May 12, 1944 (Raitt as Liliom); Block, *Richard Rodgers Reader*, 121–22 (Langner on Raitt); Rodgers, *Musical Stages*, 238 (Raitt); Sam Zolotow, "New Comedy Due by George Kelly," *NYT*, January 15, 1945 (Helburn in Hollywood; of the future cast of *Liliom*, only Bambi Linn was "set"); "Premiere Tonight of *One Man Show*," *NYT*, February 8, 1945 (Jean Darling and Eric Mattson to play "Marie" and Mr. Snow); "News of the Stage," *NYT*, February 16, 1945 (the recruiting of Clayton, a "Metro starlet"). Some contractual problems ensued over Raitt because he had signed a film contract with the Producers Releasing Corporation; D'Andre, "Theatre Guild," 219–25.

16 An early *Carousel* program (week beginning October 21, 1945) is available at www.playbill.com/production/carousel-majestic-theatre-vault-0000013229.

17 Rodgers, *Musical Stages*, 238 (easier to work); Kara Anne Gardner, *Agnes de Mille: Telling Stories in Broadway Dance* (New York: Oxford University Press, 2016), 106–7 (good relations with Mamoulian but worsening ones with Rodgers); Sam Zolotow, "33 Shows to Give Holiday Matinees," *NYT*, February 22, 1945 (*Allegro*).

18 LC/RM, Box 102, folder 4 (New Haven and Boston programs); Ferenc Molnár, *Companion in Exile: Notes for an Autobiography*, trans. Barrow Mussey (New York: Gaer Associates, 1950), 214 (past midnight); Block, *Richard Rodgers Reader*, 121–24 (Langner on the tryouts); Agnes de Mille, *And Promenade Home* (Boston: Little, Brown, 1958), 243. De Mille (followed by Fordin, *Getting to Know Him*, 233) says that half of the act 2 ballet, five complete scenes, "a couple of good songs," and "several verses in the remaining ones" were cut after New Haven, but this seems greatly exaggerated.

19 D'Andre, "Theatre Guild," 234–37 (Boston reviews); Rodgers, *Musical Stages*, 242–43, and de Mille, *And Promenade Home*, 247–48 (Roosevelt); Helen Ormsbee, "Theatre Guild Presents New Musical, *Carousel*, by Authors of *Oklahoma!*", *New York Herald Tribune*, April 15, 1945 (Molnár; see also Rodgers, *Musical Stages*, 240–41); Block, *Richard Rodgers Reader*, 123 (Langner on the dress rehearsal). Langner also noted that Rodgers was laid out on a stretcher because he had hurt his back in Boston (compare Rodgers, *Musical Stages*, 243).

## CHAPTER 4

1 On the historiographical and other problems of the "integrated" musical, see James O'Leary, "*Oklahoma!*, 'Lousy Publicity,' and the Politics of Formal Integration in the American Musical Theater," *Journal of Musicology* 31 (2014): 139–82.

2 The distinction lies at the heart of McMillin, *The Musical as Drama*, which also (134–39) has an important discussion of the music in act 1, scene 2 of *Carousel* (up to the "Bench scene") on which I variously draw below.

3 Carter, *Oklahoma!*, 25–26.

4 However, the introduction to the song in the original-cast recording has the words come instead from an embroidery sampler. This was followed in the film version of *Carousel*.

5 For Mamoulian and the staging of the opening of *Carousel*, see Mark N. Grant, *The Rise and Fall of the Broadway Musical* (Lebanon, NH: Northeastern University Press, 2004), 238–43.

6 Dominic Symonds, *We'll Have Manhattan: The Early Work of Rodgers and Hart* (New York: Oxford University Press, 2015), 289n113. Swain, *The Broadway Musical*, 109–10, relays the suggestion that for the "Carousel Waltz," Rodgers repurposed a concert waltz (*Tales of Central Park*) that was commissioned by Paul Whiteman in fall 1944 but which Whiteman never received. Whiteman certainly included Rodgers in his list of desired composers; see "Commissions Given for Radio Music," *NYT*, June 1, 1944. However, as yet the connection can be neither confirmed nor denied. As for another unproven case of Rodgers reusing music in *Carousel* ("A Real Nice Clambake" based on "A Real Nice Hayride" intended for *Oklahoma!*), see Carter, *Oklahoma!*, 285n23.

7 For who did what for the orchestration, see Steven Suskin, *The Sound of Broadway Music: A Book of Orchestrators and Orchestrations* (New York: Oxford University Press, 2009), 358–60; Don Walker thought it "the best job I have ever done" (ibid., 360). Rodgers's comment on opera is given in Meryle Secrest, *Somewhere for Me: A Biography of Richard Rodgers* (New York: Alfred A. Knopf, 2001), 275. The *Carousel* orchestra had thirty-nine players: 2 flutes (doubling piccolos), 1 oboe (doubling cor anglais), 2 clarinets, 1 bassoon (doubling bass clarinet), 3 French horns, 2 trumpets, 3 trombones, 1 tuba, 1 harp, 1 percussion, 13 violins (9 first and 4 second), 4 violas, 3 cellos, 2 double basses.

8 Rodgers's early draft for the scene then had a third verse for Billy ("Do you love me, Julie Jordan?"); see David Crews Möschler, "Compositional Style and Process in Rodgers and Hammerstein's *Carousel*" (M.A. thesis, University of California, Davis, 2010), 23–24, 26. This draft and others are in LC/RR, Box 3, folders 16–27.

9 Rodgers drafted it in C major (an easier key in which to work); the orchestration took it up a half-step. There are obvious dangers in reading too much into such choices, given that transposition was common practice to suit a given voice, but the choices were still made.

10 Möschler, "Compositional Style and Process," 28.

11 Cited in Frederick Nolan, *The Sound of Their Music: The Story of Rodgers and Hammerstein*, 2nd ed. (New York: Applause, 2002), 159.

12 Amy Asch, ed., *The Complete Lyrics of Oscar Hammerstein II* (New York: Alfred A.Knopf, 2008), 311 (melody first); Fordin, *Getting to Know Him*, 225 (first version).

13 Hammerstein, "Notes on Lyrics," 14–15; compare McMillin, *The Musical as Drama*, 63.

14 Möschler, "Compositional Style and Process," 30.

15 Rodgers, *Musical Stages*, 239–40; de Mille, *And Promenade Home*, 238. Rodgers's continuity sketch for "Soliloquy" (LC/RR, Box 3, folder 24) is reproduced in Dominic McHugh, "'I'll Never Know Exactly Who Did What': Broadway Composers as Musical Collaborators," *Journal of the American Musicological Society* 68, no. 3 (2015): 605–52, at 612–13 (the article's Fig. 1). The music clearly follows the text (some of which is cued in), and it is close to the final version save that the opening is in A minor (as it reappears later in the piece) rather than B minor (though all the other keys are the same).

16 "My little girl" was originally preceded by a kind of verse ("When I have a daughter, / I'll stand around in bar-rooms"), a late insert that was then cut and replaced by a line of speech ("I can just hear myself braggin' about her!"); Möschler, "Compositional Style and Process," 33–35. This was included in the original-cast recording, and John Raitt followed this reading in his performance for the *General Foods 25th Anniversary Show: A Salute to Rodgers and Hammerstein* (1954). It is present in the new-edition vocal score (though the cut is noted).

17 Möschler, "Compositional Style and Process," 35–37. The coda is not present in Rodgers's continuity sketch.

18 De Mille, *And Promenade Home*, 240 (cut), 243 (challenge); Gardner, *Agnes de Mille*, 107 (prologue).

19 Hammerstein, "Turns on a Carousel."

20 Carter, *Oklahoma!*, 131 (Hammerstein suspicious); de Mille, *And Promenade Home*, 239 (inserting dialogue). For the various stages in creating the ballet, see Gardner, *Agnes de Mille*, 96–105, with details of Hammerstein's outline of the ballet in his draft libretto of January 9, 1945, and of de Mille's own notes revealing how her ideas developed.

21 De Mille discusses working with Rittman in *And Promenade Home*, 62–69.

## CHAPTER 5

1 Rittenberg, "Ferenc Molnár," xvi.
2 Hammerstein, "Notes on Lyrics," 18 (bass fiddle); Carter, *Oklahoma!*, 189–90.
3 Cited in Fordin, *Getting to Know Him*, 220.
4 "Molnar Tackled by Progressive Theater Guild," *Louisville (KY) Courier-Journal*, May 1, 1921. Molnár's name was typically styled without the acute accent in US newspapers.
5 "Did Liliom Go to Heaven?" *Baltimore Sun*, June 26, 1921; Brooks Atkinson, "The Play: Burgess Meredith and Ingrid Bergman in a Revival of Ferenc Molnar's *Liliom*," *NYT*, March 26, 1940; Atkinson, "Molnar's *Liliom*: Burgess Meredith and Ingrid Bergman Appear in the Current Revival," *NYT*, March 31, 1940.
6 McGilligan, *Fritz Lang*, 199.
7 D'Andre, "Theatre Guild," 185–87.
8 Hammerstein, "Notes on Lyrics," 24–25.
9 "Demobilization Seen Challenge to Church to Offer Spiritual Guidance to Millions," *NYT*, May 22, 1944 (Bonnell); Wilbur J. Cohen and Jessica H. Barr, "War Mobilization and Reconversion Act of 1944: An Analysis of the 'George Bill,' " *Social Security Bulletin* 7, no. 10 (October 1944): 10–15, 30 (Roosevelt); "100 Years of Marriage and Divorce Statistics: United States, 1867–1967," National Vital Statistics System, ser. 21, no. 24, available online at www.cdc.gov/nchs/data/series/sr_21/sr21_024.pdf (divorce rates). See also Kati Donovan, "No One Walks Alone: An Investigation of the Veteran and the Community in Rodgers and Hammerstein's *Carousel*," *Studies in Musical Theatre* 5 (2011): 287–95.
10 Robert Brustein, "Nothing to Declare," *New Republic*, March 1, 1993, 26–28; *Congressional Record* 140, no. 55 (May 9, 1994; Senator Strom Thurmond's tribute to President Nixon).

## CHAPTER 6

1 Downes, "Roots of Native Opera" (*Porgy and Bess*) and "Broadway's Gift to Opera" (*Oklahoma!*); Stephen Hinton, *Weill's Musical Theater: Stages of Reform* (Berkeley: University of California Press, 2012), 261–68.
2 Oscar Hammerstein II, "Voices Versus Feet," *Theatre Magazine* (May 1925): 14, 70; Howard Pollack, *George Gershwin: His Life and Work* (Berkeley: University of California Press, 2006), 603–6 (reception of *Porgy and Bess*).
3 Downes, "Broadway's Gift to Opera"; B/TG, Box 77, folder "Gassner Memos 1942–3."
4 Olin Downes, "A New Opera: Rodgers' and Hammerstein's *Liliom*, after Molnar, for Early Production," *NYT*, December 24, 1944. All subsequent quotations are taken from here.

5 Lewis Nichols, "No Best Play: The Drama Critics Circle Fails to Give its Two Annual Awards," *NYT*, April 7, 1946.
6 Gertrude Samuels, "Success Story Set to Music," *NYT*, January 21, 1945; Richard Rodgers, "Our Future Musical Theater," *Etude* 63, no. 2 (February 1945): 69 (warmed-up dish; *Carmen Jones*).
7 D'Andre, "Theatre Guild," 238–39 (Rascoe, Chapman, Brown); Mark A. Schubart, "Mr. Rodgers Bypasses the Opera: Composer of *Carousel* Isn't Worrying about Theatre Trends," *NYT*, August 12, 1945. In Samuels, "Success Story Set to Music," Rodgers rather coyly hinted at writing something for a symphony orchestra "next spring."
8 D'Andre, "Theatre Guild," 173 (scaring off; from an interview between Rodgers and Warren Smith in the *Boston Post*, April 8, 1945); Stark Young, "*Oklahoma*'s Little Sister," *New Republic*, May 7, 1945, 644.
9 Thomas R. Pryor, "*Carousel* Rights Acquired by Fox," *NYT*, July 1, 1955. Twentieth Century–Fox had made a significant investment in the stage version of *Carousel*, in part because of its ownership of the film rights to the play; Sam Zolotow, "New Guild Play Opening Tonight," *NYT*, March 13, 1945.
10 Shirley Jones, *Shirley Jones: A Memoir*, with Wendy Leigh (New York: Gallery, 2013), 84–85. Jones also reports (77) having heard that Judy Garland was to play Julie Jordan in the film.
11 Gardner, *Agnes de Mille*, 109–11.
12 Daniel Rosenthal, *The National Theatre Story* (London: Oberon, 2013), 493–502.

# INDEX

CPSIA information can be obtained
at www.ICGtesting.com
Printed in the USA
BVHW080822240423
662925BV00007B/522